PERSPECTIVES ON ECONOMICS

Reflections on aspects of the changing British economic system in the context of Christian theology

The report of a Working Group of economists and theologians commissioned by the Industrial and Economic Affairs Committee of the General Synod Board for Social Responsibility

CIO PUBLISHING
Church House, Dean's Yard, London SW1P 3NZ

ISBN 0 7151 6563 1

Published for the General Synod Board for Social Responsibility
by CIO Publishing

THIS REPORT

This report is offered as a contribution to debate because its contents are thought likely to prove of interest. It is not intended to represent the policy of the Board for Social Responsibility itself.

The Board is an advisory committee of the Church of England General Synod. Its functions are to promote and co-ordinate the thought and action of the Church in matters affecting the lives of men and women in society.

The Industrial and Economic Affairs Committee, which has commissioned this report from a specially convened Working Group, is a Constituent Committee of the Board. It has among its members and regular consultants: company directors, trade union officials, university lecturers, civil servants, bishops and industrial chaplains.

The cover picture shows copies of the *TUC Economic Review*, the *CBI News* and the *Financial Times* reflected in a mirror. The picture illustrates the theme that all economic relationships come under 'the judgement of God, declared in the powerlessness of the cross and the reality of the resurrection' (paragraphs 8.11–8.13).

Photograph: Paul Brett

Printed by The Ludo Press Ltd, London SW18 3DG

FOREWORD
by the Rt Revd Simon Phipps, Bishop of Lincoln

In publishing this report, the Industrial Committee is continuing its tradition of preparing documents on significant industrial and economic issues being faced by the nation.

The report has been produced by a group of economists and theologians, meeting over two years. This has made for an interesting encounter between practitioners of disciplines which do not often enough engage in this way. The author of each individual chapter is indicated in the report, although what each has written has been shaped by substantial discussion in the group as a whole.

The aim, on this occasion, has been to be rather more descriptive and educational, than prescriptive and prophetic, in order that people may try to understand and reflect. It does not set out to support one particular approach, nor to condemn others. The report sees economics in terms of change and process rather than as something static. It is concerned with human behaviour as well as economic theory. In this country, the literature relating theology and ethics with economic issues is small and this report makes a valuable contribution in an area of increasing interest.

I would like to thank the group warmly for its work and to commend the report for widespread study in the Churches and beyond.

September 1984

SIMON LINCOLN
Chairman,
Industrial and Economic
Affairs Committee

CONTENTS

INTRODUCTION

The attention which Christians are often exhorted to give to issues of public concern can make them aware of the uncertainty of their grasp of the principles which should guide their thoughts and judgments on such matters. Nowhere is this more apparent than in the field of economic policy. For example, everyone is agreed that the present levels of unemployment in Britain are intolerable, but when it comes to doing something about them, there is a babel of conflicting advice. Not even the 'experts' can agree. Why is this? Why do the economists not speak with a single voice? Why does the Church not give a clear lead?

In the hope of shedding some light on this confused and confusing situation the Industrial and Economic Affairs Committee of the Board for Social Responsibility invited a small group of such 'experts' in economics and theology to address themselves to these basic but bewildering questions. This group met together over a period of two years and engaged in intensive discussion, theologian and economist each listening to and trying to understand the other. This report is the fruit of our discussions.

Our original hope was to produce a single document which we could all sign and which would set out clearly an agreed Christian judgment on the present economic state of affairs. This proved in the circumstances not to be possible. None of us approached the discussions from a fixed position or with a closed mind, but we soon discovered that individual assumptions and consequently individual perceptions were noticeably different. More important still, although our perceptions and understandings began to be modified as our discussions proceeded, they did not necessarily begin to merge, nor did they hold out the promise of an agreed judgment. We should have liked to write something that was prophetic as well as educational, but this double objective never came into clear focus. Moreover, the whole process in which we were participating, calling as it did for an analysis of human behaviour and institutions in a period of rapid change, turned out to be more complex and difficult than we had anticipated. The wide range of tools needed for such an analysis, which crossed neat disciplinary boundaries, was not immediately available to us, either individually or together. Furthermore, the question began to force itself upon us whether an agreed Christian judgment was in principle possible, and if it was possible, what sort of judgment it would be in the light of what our discussions had taught us.

After considerable heart-searching we concluded that we had sufficient of a common mind to be able to produce something more coherent than a symposium of independent essays. Our discussions had not been without value, despite the fact that we had not reached agreed judgments. Thus, the reflections we offer are *the outcome of our interacting with each other* and exhibit a large measure of interdependence, even though the prime responsibility for each chapter remains with the person named. Part I ('Methods and Context') concerns itself with the ways in which the economist and the theologian go about their respective tasks and the main changes which have been taking place in the economy in Britain. Part II ('Economic Institutions') is marked by a different concern and approach. Instead of attempting to adjudicate between the various economic schools and philosophies described in Part I, we have turned our attention to three areas of economic activity and influence, the business enterprise, the community of work and the state. In doing so we wished to emphasise our concern with *human* beings and *human* behaviour. The authors of chapters 5, 6 and 7 were encouraged, not only to describe economic institutions, but also to begin to evaluate them. Indeed, in this context description and evaluation cannot be kept totally apart. Part III ('Reflections') begins the task of theological evaluation by mapping out the groundwork for such an endeavour. There remains a gap, however, which still needs to be bridged, between Christian insight and moral conviction on the one hand and economic problems and practical decisions on the other. That there is such a gap in our work is undeniable. The nature of this gap–and the reason why it seems, generally speaking, to loom larger in the area of economics than in some other areas of ethical concern–itself needs further philosophical and theological analysis. It may be, among other things, that this is an area in which, as well as disagreement about practical policies, there is also a conflict of values which Christian faith as such does not immediately solve.

Some interesting features of our discussions are worth drawing attention to. First, the world of economics is not a closed world. *Economic values are not self-justifying, but need to be set in the larger context of human values.* Economists can provide a number of different solutions to economic problems, all of which may or may not 'work' in the long term. But with each solution a cost has to be paid at the social and human level, and these costs are varied and far-reaching. Consequently human beings have to make up their minds what they think human life is all about and what kind of society they wish to hand on to their children and grandchildren.

Secondly, *the Christian tradition has something important to contribute to these fundamental choices,* not necessarily by way of detailed policy and programme, but, more likely, by way of vision and insight into the God-given nature of humanity and the fulfilment which God intends for it in his kingdom. God's kingdom is a transcendent but not a purely 'other-worldly' reality. Hence its bearing on a Christian view of the way in which this world should be ordered is both critical and constructive. There is, of course, more than one way of articulating its significance. Two ideas that found some favour with us were, first, that of a widening community of free and interdependent persons and, secondly, that of a just, participatory and sustainable society. Such ideas may not immediately prescribe this or that policy in detail, but they point in certain directions and rule out others. For example, interdependence and participation stress the values of community and suggest, not that everyone should have a finger in every pie, but that everyone should have access to a shared responsibility.

Thirdly, *the methods which the economist and the theologian employ are not totally dissimilar,* despite the fact that the theologian operates within a context of revelation. Both wrestle with changing situations and try to interpret the processes of change. In seeking the best way out of trouble both move backwards and forwards between vision–or theory–and the facts of the situation. There are limits to what each can achieve, because human behaviour is never completely predictable, and in times of rapid change particular judgments and prescriptions quickly become obsolescent. They should not expect, therefore, finally to resolve the social tensions which rapid economic changes produce, but by understanding the forces which are at work they may hope to discover ways of making these tensions creative rather than destructive.

Finally, although we have not produced an itinerary for economic progress, we believe that we have drawn a *kind of map* of part of the economic terrain. We hope that *Perspectives on Economics* will be of use to a wide range of readers who wish, from a Christian starting point, to work towards their own informed judgments about the economic issues which confront the society they live in. The issues are far-reaching, and there is still much work to be done.

PETER BAELZ (Chairman)
DONALD HAY
JOHN HUGHES
JOHN PICKERING
DOUGLAS TODD
PAUL BRETT (Secretary)

Part One
Methods and Context

Chapter One
WHAT ECONOMICS IS ABOUT

Donald Hay opens the discussion, in Part One, by explaining that the maximising principle is at the heart of modern economic analysis and by describing the approaches of broad utilitarians, radical socialists and radical libertarians to questions of economic policy.

Economists in Debate

1.1 Some years ago, at the peak of the discussions about Britain's entry into the European Economic Community, some 250 economists wrote to *The Times* opposing such a step. Their assessment was that the costs of entry would outweigh the benefits to be derived. A day or two later another large group of economists wrote expressing equally firm approval for entry. Such conflicts of professional opinion are by no means uncommon. More recently the Cambridge Economic Policy Group expressed the belief that it would be possible to reduce unemployment by two million if the government pursued particular expansionary economic policies coupled with a degree of protection for British industry. But government spokesmen, echoing their economic advisers, have repeatedly said that governments cannot create jobs. There indeed seems to be something in the jibe that if you seat three economists round a table you will get at least four different views as to what should be done. This first chapter reflects on this situation, not by addressing particular issues, but by considering how most economists go about their work and in particular how they reach conclusions on policy issues.

What Economists Try to Explain

1.2 A common conception is that economics is all about money. It is not, though money has an important role in a modern economy. Economics is primarily about *resources* and the uses that people in society make of them. The word 'Resources' is taken in its very widest sense. It includes not only physical resources (land, climate, minerals) but also human resources (the size of the labour force and its skills) and constructed resources (machinery, factory buildings, office blocks, houses, roads, railways, distribution networks). These resources are combined in various ways in an economy to produce the goods and services that the community needs (or demands) for its continued existence. Some of these goods will be consumed immediately (food, haircuts); others may have a longer life (books, televisions, houses); others may simply add to the stock of productive assets (new machines, factories). But this process of production and consumption is not a mechanical one. It involves the activity of *people in society*. Their actions determine the outcomes. Hence economics is a social science. It is the economic behaviour of people that has to be explained. There is no attempt, however, to explain the behaviour of particular individuals, or to explain other equally important aspects of human behaviour. Economists are looking for the common features in the economic behaviour of groups of people. These groups may be defined in different ways (coalminers, housewives, members of the upper middle class, middle managers) depending on the particular question that is under consideration.

ECONOMIC BEHAVIOUR

1.3 The first step in economic analysis is virtually always *micro-economics*. The economist identifies different economic actors, and then tries to explain their activities and economic behaviour. Traditional analysis identifies the main economic actors as firms, which organise production, and households, which provide resources for production and then consume the proceeds. Within these broad categories further distinctions are often made, for example, between transnational corporations, nationalised firms, large quoted companies, private companies and small family firms. The financial sector is usually given separate consideration. Other institutions like trade unions, and the government itself, are also studied for their economic behaviour.

THE MAXIMISING PRINCIPLE

1.4 The dominant method of analysis is to set up a *model* of the behaviour of a particular economic actor, which can be subjected to logical and possibly mathematical development. The key economic actor in the business enterprise, for example, is the manager. His task is to pursue the objectives of the company (which may be short-run profits, profits over a long term, growth) subject to the various constraints placed on him. These may be physical (the amount of factory space available), or they may arise from the activities of other economic actors (trade unions in the supply of labour, competition with other firms in the market, the willingness of banks to finance the activities of his firm). Formal analysis of the firm is pursued by constructing a model in which the assumed behaviour and the various constraints are expressed in mathematical form, and then asking how the manager can achieve the maximum value for a chosen objective given these constraints. The assumption is then made that a rational manager will behave in the *maximising* fashion. If the model is accurate it then becomes possible to predict his behaviour when the constraints are changed (unions bargain for higher wages, competition intensifies or the bank varies its interest rate on lending).

1.5 The maximising principle is at the heart of modern economic analysis, and has been extended to all economic actors. Thus a household is thought to arrange the disposition of its resources (especially labour) and the pattern of its consumption, to maximise its satisfaction or utility. The principle has been attacked on various grounds. Some critics have denied its validity as a psychological theory; people are not the calculating rationalists they have been made out to be and the information available to them is quite insufficient for them to be able to take the maximising decisions the theory requires. Other critics have pointed to the exceptionally thin sociological basis of the theory. The objectives of particular actors reflect their class backgrounds, and the culture of their society. The image of individuals being free to make choices is an illusion. Despite the undoubted cogency of these criticisms, little has been done to provide satsifactory alternative analyses which take them into account.

INTER-CONNECTEDNESS

1.6 With micro-economics each individual actor's analysis has to take the economic environment, and hence the behaviour of all the other actors, as given. But in the real world things are not so easily isolated. If, for example, the government decides to increase the tax on petrol, the immediate effect is likely to be a decline in the quantity of petrol bought. This will have an effect on the profits of filling stations and on the petrol companies, and they may cut back production and employment. At the margin some people who would have bought cars now decide to do without, so demand for cars falls and this has other effects in the car manufacturing sector. Those who use cars less will make more use of public transport. The rise in the petrol price will also affect the cost of distribution to wholesalers and retailers generally. So some other prices to consumers will rise. The inter-connectedness, or *general equilibrium*, of the economic system is one reason why economics is so complex.

ADDING EVERYTHING UP

1.7 One method of coping with this complexity has been of particular importance to public policy in the post-war years. This is to make the assumption that particular groups of economic actors can be treated analytically *as if* they all acted in the same way. Thus all the firms are aggregated into the production sector, all the households into the household sector, all financial institutions into the financial sector. This is the basic idea behind *macroeconomic analysis*. The advantage of aggregation is that it permits attention to be focused on the links between sectors, and on the behaviour of the system as a whole. Thus households supply resources, especially labour, to firms, and receive wages and profits. Households use a part of their income to buy the goods that firms have made. Another part of the income is saved in the financial sector. Firms themselves borrow from the financial sector to finance their capital investment. The government enters the picture by levying taxes and through its own expenditure. The system can be easily extended to incorporate exports and imports and international flows of money capital. The total stock of money (cash and deposits at the commercial banks) becomes an important variable in the system. The complete system is then used to determine changes in the level of national income (the value of goods and services produced), the rate of wage and price inflation, the behaviour of the balance of payments and, of course, unemployment and employment. A change in government policies (such as a tax change) or other changes outside the system (such as the growth of overseas markets) can be traced through to estimate the final effects on these variables.

THEORY AND EVIDENCE

1.8 The models discussed above have generated three kinds of further studies by economists, The first concerns itself with pure theory, the second and third with matching the theory to the evidence.

1.9 Partly because the latter is so difficult to achieve satisfactorily, a great deal of effort has gone into developing mathematical models of the economy which require as few assumptions as possible about the actual constraints facing economic actors and about their precise response to changes in those constraints. The aim is to get results which will generalise, so that specific information is unnecessary. Abstract analysis of this kind has occupied some of the best minds in the economic profession over the past 30 years, and its academic standing in the profession is high. But there are some grounds for believing that in some areas abstraction and mathematical sophistication are being sought for their own sake. The danger is that abstraction from reality begins to distort understanding of reality itself.

1.10 The second and third kinds of studies are more closely linked to empirical reality and form the discipline of *econometrics*. The second tries to test economic theories against the evidence to see whether they are capable of explaining the phenomena. The third kind of study presumes that the theory is more or less right and concerns itself with trying to quantify the economic system (what precise effect, for example, would a one per cent change in the mortgage rate have on house prices?).

1.11 The major difficulty with testing theory directly is that economists cannot perform controlled experiments in which they can isolate the effects they wish to study. Instead the data have to be taken from the real world, where the observed values are the outcome of a very large number of contributory factors. Econometricians try to account for these other variables, but they can never be sure that they have done so satisfactorily. Hence if the facts do not fit the theory they will not know whether to reject it or whether to look around for some other factor that they failed to take into account in their examination of the evidence.

1.12 Quantification can occur at various levels, depending on the questions that have to be answered. One of the most interesting is the development of large scale computer models of the whole economy that can be used to simulate its course and, in particular, the response of the whole system to changes in government policies. These consist of a complex system of equations stored in the computer, which model the behaviour of various sectors of the economy, including their quantitative responses to changes in other economic variables. The accuracy of these predictions depends critically on whether the underlying economic theory is correct (do firms really behave in this way?), and whether the quantitative estimates are correct (will a 1 per cent drop in interest rates increase business fixed investment by ½ per cent or 4 per cent and how quickly will this increase occur?).

STATIC AND DYNAMIC

1.13 The first reason, then, why economists are often seen to be in disagreement is simply that it is not easy to decide whether the theory is correct and the quantification accurate. This is particularly the case where the performance of the whole economy is in question. One reason for this is that the analysis often maintains a static view of the social institutions that make up the economy. But in fact institutions change over time. They adjust their behaviour in the light of events. Their relative power in the economy also shifts. The economic policy of the government can itself be a powerful agent of such changes. Hence predictions that are made on the basis of *given* behaviour by *given* institutions may turn out to be quite erroneous. Economic models and methods need constant reappraisal.

1.14 One lesson to be learned from the past 30 years of policy-making in the UK is that it is all too easy in economics to be wrong. That is not, however, to suggest that economic analysis is not a worthwhile exercise. It is an important part of the attempt to understand the society in which people live. and the effects that changes have on the welfare of its citizens.

What Economists seek to Prescribe

1.15 In general, economists have not been content just to model and quantify the behaviour of the economy. They have generally also proposed solutions to economic problems. Indeed there is little doubt that this has come to be expected of them by a wide range of policy makers, politicians, civil servants and various interest groups. The preoccupation with *policy* has fed back into the kinds of analysis undertaken and the particular questions asked. When inflation is at the centre of policy debate research on inflation flourishes. A rigid distinction between analysis and policy prescription cannot thus be drawn. In the same way, economic analysis is not entirely independent of the values that the economist brings to the task.

1.16 What then is the basis for policy prescriptions that economists adopt? There are three main approaches representing broad groupings of economists.

BROAD UTILITARIANS

1.17 The first main approach is that of utilitarianism. Its most basic premise is that a particular action should be evaluated by its consequences, and not by the rightness or otherwise of the action in itself. However, most policy actions have good and bad consequences, and it is a matter of some importance how these are to be evaluated in terms of human welfare. This approach to policy is thoroughly consistent with the maximising approach of main-stream economic analysis described above. Individual economic actors seek to maximise their own advantage by acting within the system to obtain certain incomes. The policy maker then acts to regulate the economic system to maximise some social objective. The implicit assumption is that the economic system needs help to 'get it right', though the various economic institutions in society are adequate in themselves, even if they need to be influenced as to their behaviour.

1.18 The method is best explained by two examples. The first concerns monopoly policy. Two firms might announce their intention to merge, and the Monopolies and Mergers Commission would be asked to report. A very simple investigation might suggest gains and losses. A large firm would be able to realise economies of scale, it would be able to take more risks in research and development, it would be able to survive overseas competition and preserve employment in the UK in the long run. On the other hand, the larger firm would have less competition in domestic markets, might be able to raise prices in the long run, and would be likely to rationalise production by closing a plant in a high unemployment area. Should the merger be permitted to go through? The answer, on the broad utilitarian view, would be yes, if the gains outweighed the losses. This is the principle of *cost-benefit* analysis.

1.19 The second example concerns macroeconomic policy. The computer model of the economy described above might be used to provide alternative scenarios for the economy given alternative fiscal and monetary policies. The growth of the economy, the level of unemployment, the rate of inflation and the exchange rate would follow different paths. To evaluate the possibilities economists would then apply weights to different economic indicators representing their own evaluation of the contribution (or cost) to social objectives, or what they believed to be the evaluation of politicians or public opinion. Once again the objective would be to maximise some broadly defined concept of social welfare.

1.20 These two examples indicate another area where economists differ. They may agree on the consequences to be expected from a particular economic change; they may agree on a basic utilitarian method, but they may disagree about the weights to be attached to different outcomes. Thus an economist who gives greater weight to getting the inflation rate down than to ensuring full employment, will provide a different policy prescription from one who sees full employment as deserving a higher priority. The situation will of course be even more confused if they also disagree about the appropriate model of the economy!

RADICAL SOCIALISTS

1.21 A neo-Marxist critique of conventional economic policy-making would make two criticisms. The first is that the approach described above focuses attention on the wrong policy questions, with the result that the class struggle for shares in the national income, and the underlying instability of the capitalist system, are ignored. Economists' preoccupations with modelling and stabilising the economy reflect their class bias and prevent them from asking more fundamental questions about social welfare and the exercise of power in society. If they did ask these questions, they would begin to understand that economic problems cannot be solved without change in the institutional fabric of the economy. For example, the neo-Marxist analysis sees unemployment as endemic to capitalism. It can only be solved by replacing capitalist enterprise with some form of planned economy. Similarly only social ownership of the means of production will solve the conflict between capital and labour, a destabilising element in capitalist economies. Thus a neo-Marxist policy prescription will be based on a commitment to institutional change. Its advocates will look for signs of change in the economy, and will promote ways of encouraging and accelerating such change as they believe to be inimical to capitalism in the long run.

RADICAL LIBERTARIANS

1.22 The third main approach represents an increasingly influential intellectual stream in economic policy making, and has contributed to the thinking of Mrs Thatcher's administration in Britain, and Mr Reagan's administration in the United States. According to the radical libertarian approach all social arrangements, including economic institutions, should be so ordered as to maximise the freedom enjoyed by individuals in society. While a hierarchy of freedoms is acknowledged, economic freedom is given an important role as it is believed to be a precondition of certain other freedoms. Thus freedom to hold property, and freedom to work as one wishes, are prerequisites for the freedom to hold unpopular views, or the freedom to live an unconventional life. Without economic freedom, society can bring powerful (and unwelcome) economic sanctions on those who fail to conform to group mores. Similarly intellectual and religious freedoms are thought to depend on economic freedom, since it enables those with particular views to publish and distribute literature promoting their views. The particular enemy would be a state which exceeded the minimal powers entrusted to it by the populace to defend the freedom of individuals and which sought to promote its own concept of social welfare or progress. The policy prescription of libertarian radicals is quite simple. The state should as far as possible leave all economic activity to private economic actors operating in the context of a market system. Its sole concern should be to maintain competition in markets, to enforce contracts and to provide a framework of law and order within which private transactions can take place and property rights can be assured. In so far as the state is ceded the responsibility for the provision of public goods (such as defence and the administration of law) it should finance these by levying taxes which are as neutral as possible with respect to private economic activity. The government budget should balance.

VIEWPOINT AND POLICY

1.23 Given these three distinct schools of thought about the economy, it should come as no surprise that economists are frequently seen to disagree. Their particular prescriptive viewpoints will affect not only their policy recommendations, but also the topics they consider worthy of research, and even the kind of analysis that is undertaken. For example, a radical libertarian might regard the whole traditional macroeconomic apparatus for predicting the future path of the economy as irrelevant. He would argue that outcomes are not a touchstone for policy, so there is no need to bother with trying to predict them. These fundamental disagreements between economists of different persuasions are of greater importance than is generally realised, and economists have not always been ready to be honest about them in their public pronouncements. In so far as different value systems are implied in much economic analysis and policy, it is important for Christians to scrutinise them to see how they match up to their understanding of man in society and to Christian moral concepts.

Chapter Two
WHAT THEOLOGY IS ABOUT

Peter Baelz argues for the transformation of the world into something more in keeping with the kingdom of God. Although the gospel must be worked out in terms of human experience and life, he argues that it is not wedded to any specific philosophical, political, ethical or economic theory. To some it says a qualified 'yes', to others a forthright 'no', from all it removes any claim to absoluteness and ultimacy.

Theologians in Debate

2.1 If economists speak with an uncertain voice, what of theologians? Can they introduce clarity and a sense of direction where economists are divided, if not in the narrower field of practical policy, then at least in the wider context of values and goals? Something like this might be expected from Christian theologians, since they stand within a given tradition and see human life and destiny from a distinctive point of view. However, even if there is no truth in the popular notion that 'theological' considerations are irrelevant to the conduct of public affairs, it has to be admitted that theologians are seldom of one mind when it comes to the articulation and application of their faith. Why is this?

2.2 Theologians work within a tradition of faith. They accept something as 'given'. As Christians, they are persons under authority, servants of a word, communicators of a vision, disciples of a master and lord. They believe that in various ways and at various times, but supremely and normatively in the person and teaching of Jesus Christ, God makes himself known to mankind and communicates to those with ears to hear the things which belong to human salvation. There is, then, a certain *givenness* about the Christian life and faith which reflects the initiative and grace of God. On this theologians are agreed. When, however, they try to spell out in greater detail exactly *what* it is that is given, and *where* it is to be found, differences of judgment and interpretation begin to appear.

2.3 Some look first and foremost to the scriptures as the final and authoritative record of God's revelation. In matters of practice as well as of faith the Bible possesses for them a unique and unquestionable authority. They look to it for the basic principles and laws which God has laid down for the life of his human creatures. Others turn more naturally to the magisterial teaching of the Church as guardian and interpreter of the deposit of faith. For them, for example, the series of papal encyclicals, beginning with *Rerum Novarum* in 1892, develops according to its own logic the fundamental teaching of the Roman Catholic Church on social and political issues. Others, again, look in the first instance to the living tradition of the Christian community and the continuing guidance of conscience and the Holy Spirit within the moral challenge of changing situations. Judgments of right and wrong, they believe, arise out of immediate insights, which the theologian then develops into a coherent pattern. However, these are not three mutually exclusive sources. In fact theologians of every school draw from them all, although in differing ways. Thus they operate within a given context rather than with a given set of axioms. Moreover, there is no escape from the fact that all theological reflection is a form of *interpretation*. This is involved not only in the attempt to discover the original meaning of texts and traditions of the past, but also in the attempt to discern their meaning for Christian discipleship today. Such a process of interpretation is creative and dynamic rather than static and repetitive. The meaning of the scriptures for today cannot simply be read off from the page or from what they meant to Christians in the past. New situations call for new interpretations. This is not to say that theologians approach each new situation with a clean state, without referring either to scripture or to tradition. They are not slaves of their immediate context. They do not rely on isolated intuition or momentary inspiration. Nevertheless, reflecting on the circumstances in which they find themselves as well as on the tradition in which they stand, they allow each to illuminate the other, and in making their judgments they find a place for both old and new. The God to whom the scriptures bear witness is the living lord of history, not its absent architect. Theological interpretation, therefore, is less like reading an architect's plans than it is like engaging in a conversation.

What Theologians try to Do

2.4 Christian faith is God-centred. To speak of *Jesus* Christ is to speak of a man, but to speak of Jesus *Christ* is to relate that man to God. His human story becomes one with the divine story. Thus the Christian gospel sets out a way of seeing and responding to the world as *God's* world. Perception and response are two aspects of a single orientation. The world is seen as the sphere of God's continuing activity and the object of his creative and redemptive love, and in the light of this perception men and women are challenged to respond to God's presence and to participate in his purposes. Theological reflection, then, has a twofold task. On the one hand it must develop an understanding of what God is doing in and with his world. On the other hand, it must develop an understanding of what human beings can and should be doing in response to God.

THEOLOGY AND IDEOLOGY

2.5 The traditional view of the theologian's work has given to perception a certain priority over response. Hence his first task is to speak about God, his nature and purposes, and only then will he go on to speak about man's obedience, as individual and in society. What man should be about is to be determined fundamentally by what God is about. The divine character and action provide the essential criterion for evaluating human character and action.

2.6 The risk inherent in this traditional view is that theory may become divorced from action, whereas the experience of practical obedience and discipleship should be allowed to contribute to our understanding of God. The Christian's proper task, it is sometimes asserted in echo of Marx's criticism of Hegel, is not to understand the world but to change it. Action should take precedence over theory. Theories about God, the argument continues, although allegedly objective, are in fact ideologies which derive, not from God himself, but from privileged positions of power. They represent partial and distorted interests. Consequently, the conquest of ideology and the discovery of truth must be by way of action. Only a truly just society can provide the basis for a truly justifiable belief about God.

2.7 Doubtless there is an ideological element in all theological reflection. What people see is in part dependent on what they want to see. Nevertheless, Christian theology has its own resources for unmasking ideological distortion. There is an 'otherness' about the gospel of Jesus Christ which resists ideological perversion. It possesses an undeniably transcendent character and constantly questions ideological presuppositions. Thus the theological task is both critical and constructive. Moreover, it is a task which is never complete.

THE IDEA OF FREEDOM

2.8 The relation between the theological and the ideological can be illustrated by the idea of freedom. Freedom is an important and recurrent theological theme in the scriptures. It is God who liberates the children of

Israel from their bondage in Egypt. It is Jesus Christ who sets people free from the power of sin and death. Theologically speaking, then, freedom has a transcendent and universal value. God wills that men and women should enjoy the glorious liberty of his children. The essence of such freedom lies in their recognition of God as their Father and their wholehearted response to his offer of abundant life. The essence of the bondage from which God sets men and women free is their bondage to sin, whether the sin of pride, greed, fear, or something else. Now this theological idea of freedom has often been linked with other ideas of freedom, moral, political and economic. No doubt there are some links to be discerned. But sometimes the theological idea has been used uncritically to justify one or other of these non-theological ideas, simply to lend it powerful psychological support. Clearly this is a misuse of theology. It is easier, however, to be more sure about its misuse than about its proper use. At one extreme there is the danger of reducing theology to ideology, of 'politicising' the gospel. At the other extreme is the danger of making theology socially and politically vacuous, of 'spiritualising' it. Doubtless the proper use of theology will do justice to the elements of truth which are to be found in both extremes, holding them together in a creative tension without letting either dominate and destroy the other.

NATURAL AND REVEALED MORALITY

2.9 In preparing the groundwork for the practice of Christian discipleship one school of theologians emphasises the value and norms which are to be derived from reflection on what it is to be a true human being. Human nature itself, it is argued, provides the basic norms for human behaviour, for human beings function truly only when they obey the immanent laws of their own nature. Universal human values, therefore, arise out of universal human needs, and general norms for human behaviour are those which protect and foster human values. Thus Christians and non-Christians share a common moral world, and acknowledge common human virtues, such as prudence, self-control, courage and justice. The specifically Christian contribution to moral and political life does not lie in its substance, but rather in the wider context in which Christians perceive the world–it is God's world–and the deeper motive which prompts their actions–an obedient response to the divine initiative.

2.10 Another school of theologians rejects this approach more or less out of hand. Human nature, they say, is hopelessly distorted by sin. Human beings need an external authority to order their behaviour. Reason needs to be replaced by revelation. The norms for human behaviour are to be found in the scriptures. The Bible provides the divine instructions for moral and political life, whether these are, as some would argue, specific laws, or whether, as others would argue, they are more general pointers and principles.

AN ETHIC OF THE KINGDOM

2.11 There is a third approach. According to this, the Bible does not provide us with a 'revealed morality' so much as with a 'revealed reality'. It is about God's dealings with his world in nature and history, about human beings made in his image but marred by sin, and about the fulfilment of their God-given humanity in his coming kingdom. A Christian morality may indeed be grounded in what it is to be a true human being, but human nature is still in the making, distorted and incomplete, and from a Christian point of view human needs include the need of redemption and a place in God's kingdom. Hence Jesus' teaching about life in God's kingdom, and his embodiment of that teaching in his own living and dying, provide us with an ultimate criterion for assessing the variety of natural and biblical norms.

THE KINGDOM OF GOD

2.12 We shall explore this third approach in more detail, first, because of its comparative complexity, and secondly, because, in the writer's judgment, it is the most satisfactory over-all theological method.

2.13 The tension which we noted earlier between the transcendent and the secular is to be found in the interpretation of Jesus' teaching about the kingdom of God. It has been argued, on the one hand, that the kingdom of God which Jesus proclaimed was at hand was something invisible and other-worldly, bearing no relation to the kingdoms of the world. According to this interpretation Christian obedience is something intensely inward and individualistic and has nothing to do with the business of economic and political life. Such a view can be supported by this or that text when taken in isolation. But when everything that Jesus said about the kingdom is taken into account, it is difficult to avoid the conclusion that in his mind the kingdom embraced both the spiritual and the material, the inward and the outward. 'Thy kingdom come,' he taught his disciples to pray, 'Thy will be done, on earth as in heaven.'

2.14 It has been argued, on the other hand, that Jesus proclaimed a 'social' gospel, a way of ordering the whole of human life, individual and institutional, and that the Christian task is a human task of 'building' God's kingdom. But 'building' is not a word used by Jesus. His disciples were never told to build the kingdom, but to seek it, to prepare for it, and to be ready, when it came, to receive it and to enter into it. Its coming did not ultimately depend on human efforts, but on the grace and power of God.

2.15 What exactly Jesus meant when he preached that the kingdom of God was at hand, and how it would be related to the kingdoms of the world, cannot be known with certainty. However, it is likely that he believed it was being inaugurated in his own words and ministry and would be established in power, if not during his own life-time, then soon after his death. Thus the earliest Christians assumed that they too were living in the last days, and that what had begun in Jesus' life and death would shortly be completed with his manifestation in glory.

2.16 At first, members of the Christian community had little concern with the ordering of affairs in the world they knew, because they were expecting a new world to be established by God. But as time went on they had to come to terms with the fact that the history they knew had not come to an end. They had to decide to what kind of obedience God was calling them in public affairs. Such a decision became especially urgent when, in the early fourth century, the Emperor Constantine adopted the Christian faith and Christianity became the established religion of the empire. The question about the relationship between the secular city and the City of God, between the church and the world, became especially urgent.

THE TWO CITIES

2.17 Down the ages Christians have given a variety of answers to this question. At one extreme have been those who have interpreted the Christian calling in terms of a rejection of political structures based on conflicts of power and a challenge to walk the way of non-resistant, suffering love. At the other extreme have been those who have identified the church with the exercise in secular matters of a theocratic power and have not been afraid to use the secular arm in pursuit of its own religiously conceived objectives. Between these extremes, most Christian thinkers have sought in some way or other to hold together the claims both of the universal and transcendent and of the contingent and relative. Sometimes the two principles have been allowed to co-exist in an uneasy juxtaposition, represented by 'church' and 'world', and surviving on a basis of mutual non-interference. Sometimes there has been an attempt to weld them together into a single divine-human order of Christendom.

2.18 The models suggesting and supporting a particular conception of the relationship between the secular city and the city of God are numerous, but one, which may commend itself as doing greatest justice to the form of the gospel, is the model of *transformation*. The model of 'transformation' is one of those suggested by H. R. Niebuhr in his seminal study *Christ and Culture*. Here, however, it is being used in a wider sense than that intended by Niebuhr and is based on the imagery of the Transfiguration narrative and the language of Romans 12, 1-2. Hence it can include aspects of Niebuhr's other models as moments in its own realisation. According to this model the pattern and form of the kingdom of God will never be completely embodied in the world as it is, not only because of the disruptive force of human selfishness and sin, but also because of the limitations of human understanding and sympathy. Nevertheless, Christians acknowledge the reality of this pattern and power, and look to it to provide both a critique of secular life and a challenge to transform it into something more in keeping with the kingdom of God. Sometimes this challenge may lead to support of the secular authorities, at other times to tension and even conflict with them. But at all times it will bring to bear on its judgment of things as they are its vision of things as, under God's providence, they might become.

KINGDOM, CHURCH AND THE WORLD

2.19 The model of *transformation* is, admittedly, somewhat abstract. Nevertheless, it does suggest a basic orientation and approach to a Christian engagement with public affairs. It can be further developed, though still at an abstract level, by plotting the connexions between the concepts of kingdom, church and world. Some theologians have more or less identified the kingdom with the church, thus forgetting both the transcendent and universal reality of the kingdom and the human limitations of the church. In this way the power of the kingdom is restricted and debased, while the image of the church is idealised and distorted. Others have more or less identified the church with the world, thus aligning the church as one secular power in competition with other secular powers. However, neither of these approaches does justice to the richness and complexity of the Christian belief and commitment. A more dynamic model is needed.

2.20 *God's kingdom*, or rule, is transcendent and universal. The whole world is his, and although in his creative purpose he allows it an autonomy and independence of its own, it never falls outside his providential care and concern. Thus his authority extends over the whole world, and not only over the church. His rule, therefore, takes on a double aspect. In the church he rules by his word of judgment, mercy and love, and those who hear his word respond in faith and acknowledge his grace. Outside the church, however, even where there is no acknowledgment of faith, his rule is expressed in the essential dynamics of human life. It is real even though it is unrecognised. It expresses itself in a general providence. Human beings, for example, have certain basic needs. In meeting these needs they come together in some form of association. Self-interest as much as any sentiment of humanity brings them together and prompts them towards some system of power, law and order, and even some regard for justice. The institutions they create are ambiguous. They can either tyrannise or protect. But they are essential to human life. Thus in the world at large God exercises his hidden rule through the human need for peace and harmony, through the uses of power, law and order to protect societies from violence and anarchy, and through the motivation of an enlightened self-interest. But his kingdom will manifest itself in its fulness, and his rule will be universally recognised and welcomed, only when the powers and structures of the world as we know it give place to the life and power of 'the world to come'.

2.21 *The church* is called by God to be an effective sign in the world of the presence and promise of his kingdom. Its given task is to work and pray for the coming of God's kingdom and to bear witness to its present power in the lives of its members. It is to be a community of faith, hope and love, a fellowship of those who have been reconciled to God and to one another, accepting each other because all are children of God rather than because of any shared interest. Its life is to be lived in the spirit of Jesus Christ, and it is to be both salt and light to the world. But because its members are subject to the limitations of all human beings, and because, in spite of the reality of God's forgiveness, they remain entangled in the web of sin, the church must never identify itself with the kingdom. Nor should it deceive itself into thinking that it is the sole focus of God's activity and the sole object of his care. Rather, the whole of humankind, indeed the whole of creation, remains the object of God's loving care. The church is the company of those who through God's grace have come to see the world as centred in him, and whose existence is being transformed by the light of this truth.

2.22 *The world* is first and foremost God's world. But it is his world in the making, it is not yet the world as he intends it to be. Into the making God has written a large element of autonomy and independence. He makes the world chiefly by allowing it to make itself. It is an evolutionary world, a world of change, of trial and error. The dynamics of survival are built into its fundamental processes. At the human level, these dynamics become the competing claims of self-interest, both of individuals and groups. Self-interest generates various forms of social solidarity. Thus it can move the individual beyond his narrow self. But self-interest oftens turns into selfishness and sin, in the case of groups as well as individuals. The human world is a 'fallen' world, even if there was never a period of human history 'before' the fall. Hence the conflict arises between God's 'kingdom' and his 'world'. Even so, the world cannot wholly reject God's rule and authority. In order to survive, mankind needs to restrain the excesses of selfishness through the processes of government, law and order and, on the basis of self-interest if for no other reason, to promote the common good. In the world self-interest may remain the driving force, but self-interest itself comes to recognise the value of harmony and justice, at least in the sense of fairness. In William Temple's often quoted words, 'The art of government in fact is the art of so ordering life that self-interest prompts what justice demands.' But self-interest is not enough for human salvation. Hence in Jesus Christ and his church God calls his human creatures to learn the dynamic of self-giving and sacrifice.

2.23 It must be emphasised that these concepts of 'kingdom', 'church' and 'world' are *abstract* concepts, and do not denote any particular group or groups of people. They are to be understood in a dynamic way. They are intended to illustrate, from a Christian perspective, the human condition and to suggest some of the basic forces which determine it.

THE GOSPEL AND THE HUMAN SITUATION

2.24 As this model is developed further, it becomes clear that the Christian gospel cannot be divorced from the way in which human life is organised economically and politically. Nor can it be translated directly into a political ideology or an economic programme. Although the gospel must be worked out in terms of human experience and life, it is not wedded to any specific philosophical, political, ethical or economic theory. These have their own basic assumptions and criteria. The gospel, on the other hand, expresses an interpretative vision, whereby it brings these assumptions and criteria under judgment. To some it says a qualified 'yes', to others a forthright 'no', from all it removes any claim to absoluteness and ultimacy. It points to what is, and remains, transcendent. God is other than the world, even though he is fully committed to the world. This mystery of divine transcendence in our midst is one of the essential features of Christian proclamation. Because God does not abandon the world, Christians dare not abandon it.

The Gospel and Public Affairs

2.25 When Christians turn their attention from the gospel to engagement with public affairs, they have to recognise the reality both of the vision of the coming kingdom of God, for which they have been taught to work and pray, and also of the existing structures and forces of the world. Sometimes these two realities overlap, as when there is a common concern for justice; at other times they move apart, as when the principle and practice of sacrificial concern stand over against the principle and practice of self-interest. The relation between the two realities is dialectical. Unless Christians remove themselves entirely from the business of public affairs, they cannot ignore either reality. If a model of *transformation* is accepted, they will judge the reality of the world in the light of the reality of the coming kingdom. Often what is wrong and intolerable, and therefore must be opposed, is clearer than what is humanly desirable and politically possible, but they will endeavour to change public institutions and structures to bring them nearer to the demands of the kingdom. The vision which Christians have of God's kingdom is no distant dream, but at one and the same time critical and constructive. It subjects human kingdoms to a searching judgment and seeks to transform them, as far as possible, according to its pattern.

THE PATTERN OF JESUS

2.26 The characteristics of the coming kingdom of God are portrayed by Jesus in his own doings and sufferings, by parable, teaching and example. He is not directly concerned with the world of claim and counter-claim, of conflict, compromise and consensus. He declares the fundamental character and purposes of God, and summons us to reflect in our own lives the love and truth of the one whom he calls Father. He does not so much give us principles to emulate or rules to obey as set before us a way and a life.

2.27 Scripture, tradition and experience together provide Christians with resources for giving flesh to the vision within the limitations set by the situation in which they find themselves. The scriptures have a special power and authority. In them Christians have at different times found images to inspire their thought (such as creation, trusteeship, brotherhood, liberation), or principles to guide their action (such as loving-kindness, mercy, forgiveness, reconciliation), or laws to govern their behaviour (such as those against murder, lying, adultery, theft). The theological problem has always been that of providing criteria for their selection and use, and a method of interpreting their significance for the present day and age.

2.28 The theologian's contribution to the understanding of economic problems can best be seen by looking at the way in which the gospel, operating on a number of different levels, such as orientation, attitude, principle, objective, policy, etc., *comes to influence Christian action as a whole*. These levels cannot be arranged in a neat logical order, so that one could argue deductively from one level to another. Nevertheless, if the theological contribution is to be thorough and consistent, it should express an over-all harmony, a 'fittingness' of the various parts as they form a coherent whole.

VALUES, ATTITUDES AND ACTION

2.29 Fundamentally, the gospel determines the Christian's basic orientation of faith, hope and love. This orientation has then to find expression in increasingly concrete ways, in attitudes, value-judgments, objectives and decisions. It will suggest certain values for personal and communal life and foster certain attitudes and concerns. It will seek to establish certain goals, determine priorities and set objectives. It will propose policies and, at the most concrete level, make certain decisions and undertake certain actions. At every level Christians will seek to be faithful and obedient to their vision of God's kingdom. But their response will not be uniform. As they proceed from level to level there will be room for honest disagreement and need for individual judgment. Between the initial vision and the ensuing action there is more than one set of connexions which Christians may make. Sharing the same vision, they will not necessarily share the same response.

2.30 Thus there is unlikely to be one 'Christian' answer to the detailed practical problems of politics and economics. But Christians must be prepared to think through particular issues in terms of the values, attitudes and action which the vision of the kingdom of God suggests. Sometimes agreement may be reached at the relatively concrete level of policy, at other times it may be possible only at the relatively abstract level of principle and goal. But this does not imply that the outcome will always be a preservation of the *status quo*, or a compromise on some unsatisfactory middle ground. The tension between the claims of the kingdom of God and the claims of enlightened self-interest, whether of an individual, a group or a nation, is a dynamic one. The idea of 'transformation' has room for both gradual process and sudden change.

Chapter Three

THE DYNAMICS OF CHANGE IN MODERN ECONOMIES

John Hughes offers an analysis of the current economic situation and how Britain has been affected, and describes how the problems of development and displacement have constrained the continued growth of welfare services and brought a growing gap between the numbers seeking work and the jobs available.

Creation and Destruction

3.1 The previous two chapters have referred to the dynamic nature of social institutions and to the idea of transformation of the world into something more in keeping with the kingdom of God. These arguments presuppose a world that is changing and developing. In economic affairs it sounds both comforting and encouraging to be able to talk of 'development' and 'progress', but in reality it is not so simple. Progress in the production of commodities for commercial markets has in practice gone hand in hand with displacement, decline, or indeed destruction. This becomes all the more evident if the rate of change (in new products, improved processes, new centres of production and commerce, or radically new technology) accelerates, as it does when powerful firms, deploying large sums of capital and advanced technology, operate competitively in world markets.

3.2 There are three ways in which such progress and development may operate in a double-edged fashion and bring also decline and displacement.

3.3 Innovation and progress in new products and processes may operate, often with some force, as a result of the research and development budgets of big companies which themselves sometimes receive help from national governments. Such new products and processes push aside the previous generation of products and processes and may displace part of their associated capital equipment, production plant, labour force and skills. Schumpeter, a twentieth century economist, has captured this dynamic force in the phrase *creative destruction*.

13.4 Some part of twentieth century economic progress rests, secondly, upon what has been called a 'robber' economy, using up, without necessarily replacing, world resources. In some cases finite resources are directly displaced, as with mineral extraction, or there may be damage to the environment and the ecological balance.

3.5 Thirdly, through competition and trade and the workings of the market place, the development of new production centres may reduce some or all of the market share of old centres of economic activity in other locations. This trend may be additionally encouraged where established enterprise is, understandably, expected to share in the financing of public activity (such as defence or welfare state expenditure), or is required to meet high standards of safety, health and environmental control. The last decade in particular has seen a slowing of industrial growth in many European countries and a high rate of development in a number of Asian countries.

3.6 In both human and material terms progress of this double-edged kind may be difficult to handle even if the development broadly matches the displacement. But there is no guarantee of any such balancing of gains and losses. Instead, what may become established (in particular regions, or particular countries, or even more widely) is a cumulative concentration of these forces of development, and in other centres a combination of factors making for displacement and decline. Such processes may lead to the emergence of inequalities in regional development and employment, and in differences between nations in levels of economic development and rates of growth or decline. On this view, development and under-development, development and decline, may be causally linked rather than separate phenomena.

THE PACE SETTERS

3.7 Although small businesses play an important role as innovators, the main pace setters in competitive progress are large-scale, technologically-advanced enterprises. Their total material and financial resources and capacity for research and development can be very large indeed. Many of these enterprises are likely to be transnational in their scope and in the strategic deployment of their resources. Such transnational corporations are particularly important among the largest firms in the UK (whether their headquarters are here or elsewhere). Enterprises of this kind can concentrate resources on particular developments in what seem to them the most favourable locations. Both development and displacement may be accentuated in the competitive development of such enterprises, and development and displacement may be concentrated in different countries and regions.

Instability

3.8 Important elements of tension have also long been a feature of the *growth* path of commercial economies; economies have moved through clearly defined cycles of output and trade, with alternating phases of expansion and recession. In the last decade or more the international business cycle has been more strongly marked and the increased openness of modern economies to world trade has made it more difficult for individual national economies to insulate themselves from these cycles. This has posed problems of policy for national governments and for international economic action.

3.9 For the industrial countries these cycles have involved some fluctuation in industrial output and employment. Thus the industrial production of the USA rose by 30 per cent between the slump year of 1975 and the peak year of 1979. By the end of 1982 it had fallen by more than 10 per cent from that peak. In the UK, manufacturing output fell 10 per cent between 1973 and 1975, then rose by only 4 per cent in the expansion phase of the trade cycle between 1975 and 1979, to fall by 15 per cent from 1979 to 1981. This experience contrasted noticeably with the stability of the 1950s and 1960s.

3.10 There are difficulties for individual countries seeking to offset the depression stage of the business cycle by a deliberate expansion of their own internal demand for goods and services. If they are heavily involved in overseas trade (as many European countries are), and not using deliberate protectionism, they have soon been faced with disproportionate increases in imports. In face of the problems created for such countries by a shift to a deficit in their foreign payments, they have been unwilling to expand vigorously out of depression.

INFLATION

3.11 This dilemma might be reduced or resolved if a number of industrial countries (e.g. European countries) decided to co-ordinate their economic policies to expand demand and output. However, more or less simultaneous changes in output (in either direction, up or down) by the industrial countries as a whole may have important consequences for primary producers and for those countries that are heavily dependent on such exports. This is particularly true of changes in commodity prices caused by major changes in demand. Thus, the bunching of high growth rates by virtually all the major industrial countries in the early 1970s triggered a large increase in primary product prices; indeed, such prices on average doubled in little more than a year in 1972–73. This was one of the causes of the high inflation rates of the last decade.

3.12 The instability and inflation stemming from the last two trade cycles were also accentuated by large increases in oil prices introduced by the

OPEC group of producers. In each case OPEC's action took advantage of a period of substantial industrial growth and higher demand for oil. Thus, as two successive trade cycles approached their peak a steep increase in oil prices reinforced world inflation of costs and prices. The oil price increases redistributed real incomes, reducing the ability of non-oil producers to continue to expand, and throwing their foreign trade into deficit as a result of the increased cost of oil imports.

RETREAT FROM GROWTH

3.13 But if these have been the problems arising from cyclical growth, the world also has the unpleasant experience of the *retreat* from such growth. Defensive responses by industrial countries to oil price shocks have included depression of home demand, high interest rates and other measures, and have led to plant closures and large-scale unemployment. Particularly intense pressures have been felt by many less-developed countries. The slump has meant a fall in demand and often a steep fall in price for primary products. But these countries have also suffered from the high cost of imported oil and from reduced market opportunities for their manufactured exports. Having borrowed heavily to finance their development programmes, and their growing trade deficits, they have also encountered higher costs of servicing increasing debt because of high interest rates. Default on borrowing and the re-organisation of debt payments in an atmosphere of crisis have been widespread. All these combined pressures have been deepening and prolonging the recession stage of the business cycle in the early 1980s.

3.14 Hesitancy on the part of the most powerful economies about renewing concerted growth has also generated other problems. Slow growth in the major economies has implied the long continuation of 'semi-slump' conditions, with unused industrial capacity, associated constraints on renewed investment in productive capacity and large-scale, persistent, and (for the displaced workers) long-term unemployment. Curtailed demand for primary products has cut back the income and purchasing power of less-developed countries. Postponement of investment needed to bring forward additional primary product output has set up further barriers to sustained world economic development.

PROTECTIONISM

3.15 In such a context and in the absence of major international initiatives, the openness of national economies to international trade and finance has led to evident tensions. There are important benefits from an extended world division of labour. But the associated economic insecurity and displacement, in many countries, of productive capacity and employment, together with the shock waves of price and currency instability, have generated demands for national 'protection'.

3.16 It is difficult, however, to envisage any constructive solutions resulting from a widespread recourse to what has been called 'beggar my neighbour' remedies for development problems on the part of individual national economies. One country's curbed imports are another country's curbed exports. Retaliation on trade protectionism is more easily launched than stopped. The breakdown in any adequate international order for the management of currencies has in the last decade or more led to more frequent recourse by national governments to competitive devaluation. Although floating exchange rates mean that devaluation as such is not possible, it can be 'engineered' by governments, though this is not necessarily easy. The result of this breakdown has been retaliation, widening instability, and higher inflation.

The Welfare Economy

3.17 Increasingly, these problems of development and displacement, of cyclical growth and decline, have brought constraints on the continued growth of the welfare services of many industrial economies. The internal transfers to finance collectively provided public services (education, health, environment) and personal benefit payments to the dependent population, have become more difficult to manage and have come under political challenge.

3.18 Thus in Europe in the 1950s and 1960s an enlarging system of welfare services and transfer payments was financed without undue strain from the increasing taxable capacity of expanding economies and rising real incomes in the market sector. Slower growth in manufacturing (or actual decline) since 1973, associated falls in employment and lessened profitability, have served not only to curb tax revenues but also to raise state spending on benefit payments and on aid to industry. Limited growth in personal real incomes, and tension over pay fixing in both public and private sectors, have made more difficult any consensus over higher taxation to finance increased state spending and transfer payments. In some countries the enlargement of state military expenditure has further accentuated the tension over public finance and welfare provision in the economy.

3.19 In consequence, in some countries the human and social problems and increased inequality of economic conditions stemming from both instability and displacement effects in the commercial economy, have not been offset by an enlargement of public welfare provision, though in the OECD industrialised countries 'automatic stabilisers' have operated so that transfers now represent a larger proportion of national income than in the 1960s.

Development and Crisis in Britain

3.20 Many of these problems of economic displacement became evident in the 1920s and 1930s in a number of Britain's 'first industrial revolution' industries (such as coal, textiles, shipbuilding). More recently, displacement of market share, closure of plants and displacement of workers has affected many sectors of UK manufacturing and other industries. Britain has witnessed too the concentrated effects of such decline in particular regions, in urban-industrialised areas, in the displacement of old labour force skills and in unemployment. Such problems are compounded where labour and resources shed by some industries as they introduce more efficient processes cannot be absorbed in new industries and products because these have failed to develop in the national economy and are instead developing elsewhere in the world.

3.21 In the UK the pressures constraining economic growth and leading to large-scale decline in output in many industries and displacement of employment have appeared in the last decade in a more intense way than in most other European countries. Nevertheless, many of them are now also affected by slower growth, surplus industrial capacity and rising unemployment.

3.22 British manufacturing industries have particularly experienced the impact of changing economic conditions. Indeed, over the last decade manufacturing output has actually fallen, something unprecedented since the industrial revolution. The decade to the early 1970s was the last to exhibit a growth in output (of around one-third, an expansion rate similar to all the decades since the 1930s). From the early 1970s to the early 1980s there has been an overall decline, over 10 per cent from 1972 to 1982. The table below sets out the contrast in industrial output over two successive decades for manufacturing industries.

3.23 Other dimensions of this industrial decline may be illustrated by the fact that over two and a half million fewer workers are currently employed in UK manufacturing industries than at the start of the 1970s (a fall of 30 per cent). Moreover, despite the slow growth of the UK economy, the traditional surplus on overseas trade in manufactured goods had disappeared by 1983 in face of disproportionate increases in imports, and been replaced by a large deficit (of £2 billion).

3.24 In human terms the UK has presented in recent years an extreme example of reduction in employment and of a growing gap between the numbers seeking work and the jobs available. In the 1980s there has so far been a fall of two million in the total number of employees in employment. The displacement of manual work has been particularly acute and the registered unemployment of manual workers (over two million) represents a surplus of around 25 per cent compared with the still diminishing number of full-time jobs for these workers. These processes of decline are also regionally concentrated. Six of the major regions of Britain now have male unemployment rates close to 20 per cent.

UK MANUFACTURING (NEW DEFINITIONS) CHANGES IN OUTPUT BY DECADES

Sector:	*1962-72*	*1972-82*
Metals	(+9%)*	−28%
Other minerals and mineral products	+53%	−19%
Chemicals	+84%	+17%
Man-made fibres	+182%	−54%
Metal goods not elsewhere stated	(+19%)*	−41%
Mechanical engineering	+26%	−16%
Electrical and instrument engineering	+65%	+15%
Motor vehicles and parts	+44%	−39%
Other transport equipment	−14%	+3%
Food	+19%	+6%
Drink and tobacco	+50%	+12%
Textiles	+32%	−39%
Clothing, footwear	+16%	−17%
Paper, print, publishing	+27%	−10%
All other (including timber, furniture, rubber, plastics)	+55%	−16%
Total	+34.7%	−11.5%
Energy Industries:		
Mineral Oil Processing	+77%	−21%

*Old definition: New series not given in source.

Source: National Income 1983 Edition, Table 2.3.

INFLATION

3.25 Nor has British experience of *inflation* been a helpful one. Over the ten years to the early 1980s, UK inflation averaged some 4 per cent per annum more than the average for OECD countries. In other words, the shock waves of the two major oil price increases (in 1973–74 and 1979–80) were amplified in Britain but better handled by many of our competitors. Sluggish growth in productivity played a part. So did unresolved tensions in determining income (corporate and labour) and in the handling of public finance. Devaluation of sterling (e.g. from 1972 to 1976) in an effort to maintain competitiveness only fed further inflation of import costs into the economy. Only since 1983 has the inflation rate in Britain proved no higher than in the OECD as a whole.

MANAGING THE TRANSFERS

3.26 The UK offers too an example of the growing difficulty in managing the transfers required to sustain both a ramified system of public welfare services and the benefits needed by a dependent population much enlarged by unemployment. At the beginning of the 1970s there were 20 million people working in the production of marketed or 'traded' goods and services. This compared with five million either working in the non-traded public services (such as health and education) or unemployed. The ratio was four to one (20 million compared with five million). More recently official figures indicated a fall to around 17½ million working in the trading industries and services, compared with over eight million either working in non-traded public services or unemployed claimants. The ratio has become a little over two to one. It hardly needs to be emphasised that the problems of public finance, and of the political aspects of the levels of taxation involved, have become more difficult and more socially contentious as these ratios have shifted in this way. It is not surprising that with the change in the earlier economic balance between a growing industrial economy and a substantial and enlarging welfare state has come more disagreement about the economic and the welfare aspects of the role of the state, and about the style of economic management of a modern democracy.

Chapter Four
THE SOLUTIONS ECONOMISTS OFFER

Donald Hay describes three major schools of economic policy: Monetarist, Keynesian and New Cambridge, and argues that implicit in these policy options are profound political and ethical questions about the kind of society in which people may wish to live.

Schools of Economic Thought

4.1 The previous chapter offered an analysis of the nature of change in economic life with reference to the situation in the UK. The point was made that this needs to be set in the context of depression in the world as a whole. What can be done about this? This chapter describes the main schools of economic thought which compete with each other to offer analysis and prescription for the management of the economy of today. In the 1960s there was broad agreement between economists and policy makers about the management of the economy. All operated with a broad Keynesian view of the workings of the macroeconomy. In the 1970s, however, the previous consensus began to break down. Part of this was due to the impression that Keynesian policies had not performed very well. Part was due to the restatement of political and social objectives.

4.2 Hence there exist at least two schools of thought about macroeconomic policy, besides the Keynesian. One of these is *Monetarism* and the New Classical economics. Professor Milton Friedman has been the most persuasive advocate of the monetarist view. The New Classical view is a direct intellectual descendant of Friedman's economics, though it is more sophisticated in its analysis and is developing fast in the technical literature. In Britain this school of thought has been vigorously espoused by Professor Patrick Minford at Liverpool University. It is not clear how far it has already affected policymakers. At the other extreme, there is the ultra-Keynesian *New Cambridge* school of economic policy, developed by Professor Wyn Godley and others at the Department of Applied Economics at Cambridge. The *Moderate Keynesian* school is represented in Britain by the National Institute for Economic Research, which maintains a Keynesian analysis and policy prescription in its influential quarterly Review. At the risk of some caricature, these three positions on economic policy can be related to political groupings. Thus the Monetarist/New Classical view is close to that of the Conservative Government, though some of the 'wets' are more Keynesian in their outlook. The Moderate Keynesian view is also espoused by the Liberals, the SDP and the 'right-wing' of the Labour Party, and represents the broad central position in British politics. The New Cambridge view has clearly had an important impact on the official policy of the Labour Party. Each of these is briefly described, before an assessment is made.

Moderate Keynesianism

4.3 The intellectual origin of Keynesianism is J. M. Keynes' work *The General Theory of Employment, Interest and Money* published in 1936. There is still a great deal of disagreement about the correct interpretation of this seminal work, with an influential group of commentators arguing that Keynesianism as it developed in the 1950s and 1960s was a perversion of Keynes' original contribution.

4.4 The Keynesian position can be summed up in the sentence: *markets work but they need help*. They work in the sense that Keynesians accept that the operations of private enterprise in markets are for the most part an efficient method of allocating society's scarce resources. However, two particular sets of imperfections require action. First, most industrial markets are dominated by large oligopolistic firms, which confront monopolistic trade unions. The results are all kinds of rigidities and inflexibilities. These mean that the economic system is slow to change to new shocks and stimuli. Prices are not very flexible and outputs adjust slowly. The second imperfection is that a capitalist economy is not good at allocating resources over time, because of lack of information. Investment and savings decisions taken on the basis of private information are inadequate, because firms and persons can only operate on the basis of their 'expectations' (hunches, guesses) about the future state of the economy. Because of these imperfections, judicious intervention by the authorities is necessary, not to replace markets, but to help them out.

INTERVENTION

4.5 The form of that intervention has come to involve two elements. The first is the regulation of aggregate demand in the economy by fiscal and monetary policy. Fiscal policy involves the tax and expenditure decisions of the Government. A reduction in income tax, for example, will stimulate consumer expenditure, and the Government can add to demand directly by its own expenditure on goods and services. Monetary policy seeks to influence the spending behaviour of households and the investment of firms, by affecting the terms under which they can obtain credit. The objective is to keep aggregate demand growing smoothly at the same rate as the underlying growth in productive potential of the economy, and to avoid booms and slumps. This has a threefold effect. It prevents the emergence of unemployment in the economy. It provides a stable environment in which business has the confidence to invest for the future, and hence aids the growth rate, and it helps to stabilise the external balance and the exchange rate by ensuring that the economy does not consume more than it produces. If, however, the exchange rate is inappropriate, Keynesians are prepared to intervene in the foreign exchange market to change it. For a long time, Keynesians also thought that fiscal policy and monetary policy were sufficient to deal with the problem of inflation. Their argument was based on an empirical 'trade-off' between the rate of wage inflation and the level of unemployment. Less demand in the economy would lead to a reduction in the output of firms, which in turn would lay off workers. The growth of unemployment would lead workers to accept lower wage settlements. Firms' costs, and hence prices, would grow more slowly and the inflation rate would thus fall. In the late 1960s however it was thought that this trade-off had broken down, and there was therefore more interest in direct intervention in the workings of the labour market by means of an incomes policy.

4.6 For Keynesians the problems today are seen to be the outcome of the present instability of the world capitalist system. The first shock was the breakdown of the Bretton Woods system of fixed international exchange rates in the early 1970s. The second was the effect of the oil price rise from 1974 onwards, which created severe balance of payments problems for most of the Western economies. The third was the attempt by Western governments to solve this problem by cutting aggregate demand at home. The overall effect was a fall in aggregate demand and a sharp downward revision by businessmen of their expectations, leading to a cut in investment. The result was a downward spiral of output and employment into the worst recession since the 1930s.

POLICIES

4.7 The Keynesian policy prescription would be for a gentle expansion of aggregate demand via tax cuts and public expenditure to give business sufficient confidence about future demand for investment and new employment. However, it is dubious whether this could be achieved in one country alone. Any expansion in the UK would be likely to generate a rapid growth of imports and hence a deterioration in the balance of payments. A mild devaluation of the pound would not be unwelcome since it would also provide an incentive for exports. But this would be unlikely to be sufficient. The best solution would be for all the Western economies to reflate simultaneously thus reviving world trade and world demand generally. In so far as reflation brought about a renewal of inflationary pressures in the economy, the Keynesian policy would involve some form of incomes policy (preferably a permanent institution) to curb the power of large trade unions seeking excessive wage settlements. A vigorous anti-monopoly policy would also encourage competition and keep prices down.

4.8 Moderate Keynesians are also committed to the welfare state. Their analysis of the market economy includes the observation that people may, through no fault of their own, be unable to earn sufficient to maintain a reasonable standard of life. Unemployment, prolonged illness and old age may be the cause of poverty. So moderate Keynesians would seek to provide a safety net of cash benefits and other benefits in kind (such as medical care), paid for by progressive taxation on the better-off.

Monetarism

4.9 The fundamental proposition of monetarism is that *markets work if they are left unhindered and uncontrolled*. Problems arise when governments attempt to intervene, or when markets are monopolised. The policy implications are best seen in contrast with Keynesianism. First, employment and output are determined both in the long-run and in the short-run by the individual decisions of entrepreneurs, workers and consumers. Hence attempts by the authorities to influence the level of aggregate demand are doomed to failure. Fiscal policy (the adjustment of taxes and government expenditure) has no demand effects since government expenditure merely 'crowds out' private sector activities without increasing output or employment at all. Monetary policy to expand the economy also has no real lasting effect. In an open economy like that of the UK, an expansionary monetary policy spills over immediately into greater demand for imports. Hence the exchange rate depreciates and the prices of all traded goods (the prices of which are determined in world markets, not domestic markets) adjust by the full amount of the devaluation. Indeed people may come to understand this process so well that they will make it the basis for their expectations of price changes and adjust prices directly. The result is merely domestic inflation.

POLICIES

4.10 The policy outline would therefore be simple. Government involvement in the economy would be reduced to the minimum and confined to goods and services that are genuinely public (such as national defence, which could scarcely be provided by private markets). These would be financed by taxes that would interfere as little as possible with the functioning of private markets. A fixed rate for the expansion of money and bank credit would be determined so that the money supply increased no faster than was required by the growth in the output of goods and services in the economy. Preferably control of the money supply would be removed from Government, since governments are tempted to finance expenditure by monetary expansion, rather than by the less popular means of raising taxes. Finally, a vigorous anti-monopoly policy directed as much at trade unions as at firms would be pursued.

4.11 Since a monetarist policy has been the hallmark of the Conservative government, it is pertinent to ask how monetarists would explain Britain's current ills. They point to the long period of inflation the country has experienced, which has built up inflationary expectations among workers. Time is needed for more 'realistic' attitudes to be established in wage bargaining and this is being hindered by the trade unions. The adjustment to a lower growth rate of the money supply takes time. It also takes time for private initiative to move into the gaps left by the reduction in public activity, though this will occur in the long-run. In the meantime, some unemployment of resources is regrettable, but inevitable.

New Cambridge

4.12 The New Cambridge philosophy takes as its starting point a conviction that private markets are incapable of solving the problems of the UK economy. *Markets don't work without a great deal of help*, and in many circumstances it may be better to replace them with alternative mechanisms for resource allocation. They should be retained as servants of the allocative process, not as masters of it.

4.13 The New Cambridge position is ultra-Keynesian, so it shares with the Keynesians the analysis of the fundamental defects of the capitalist system. Inflexible product markets dominated by large firms, and the lack of information to guide investment, are again the problems. But the proposed solutions to these problems are more radical. Thus growth needs to be 'planned', with the authorities taking a policy view on which sectors are to be developed. The 'instruments' of planning include the nationalisation of industries (with co-ordinated investment planning in the whole of the public sector), planning agreements with large private sector corporations to make them more responsive to national needs, and the control of the financial sector in order to direct financial resources to investment in particular areas. With this foundation for long-run growth, the authorities would then use fiscal and monetary policy in Keynesian fashion to maintain full employment of resources. Any balance of payments problems would be dealt with by import controls as well as devaluation. Inflation is put down to external cost-push factors (the oil price rise), and to the pricing policies of big firms, rather than to trade unions. Workers are thought to seek a target *real* wage growth of 1–2 per cent per annum in line with the long-run growth of productivity and cannot therefore be blamed for inflationary pressures.

POLICIES

4.14 The policy prescription for Britain then follows immediately. The problem is deficient demand, as in the Great Depression. One solution, forcefully advocated by Cambridge economists until 1983, could be to expand aggregate demand rapidly by a mixture of tax cuts and increased government expenditure on social goods (such as health and education). A flood of imports would be avoided by import restrictions, so that demand would be directed to domestic producers. Employment and productivity would rise in the boom, enabling the real wage aspirations of workers to be met easily and avoiding a wage explosion. There would be a strong emphasis on a planned revival of the UK industrial base, using the North Sea oil resources for planned investments. The methods would involve, as explained above, nationalisation, planning agreements with major firms and the creation of a state investment bank.

Assessing the Schools

4.15 In assessing these schools of thought a number of questions may be asked, about technical matters, about political will, and about the sort of long-term vision of society which each school presupposes.

TECHNICAL MATTERS

4.16 It should be clear from this brief exposition of the various schools of thought, that there are sharp divergences about certain technical issues. Three of these may be highlighted.

4.17 First there is the question of the behaviour of wages and their part in the inflationary process. The New Cambridge school postulates 'target real wage growth' behaviour with compensation for past inflation and some addition to give an increase in the real wage over time. Keynesians believe that wage demands are influenced by the level of unemployment, incorporating some forward-looking allowance for expected inflation. Trade unions are not entirely neutral in this process. Monetarists, on the other hand, see inflation purely as a monetary phenomenon. Wages follow the trend of prices, they do not create it. Trade unions are not to be held responsible for inflation (though they come under severe criticism for their restrictive practices). A second question concerns the effectiveness of fiscal and monetary policy. Monetarists believe that any action by the authorities will eventually stimulate precisely offsetting effects in the private sector ('crowding out'). Keynesians and New Cambridge disagree and see substantial scope for policy to influence the course of the economy. A third question concerns the relative efficiency of private and planned systems in providing for the future via investment. There is no certainty that, as monetarists assert, releasing the private sector from controls and state intervention would generate faster economic growth.

4.18 Unfortunately, for the reasons outlined in chapter one, clear answers to these questions are not generally forthcoming. One possibility is that there exists no definite answer, however good the analytic tools. For example, the behaviour of economic actors can change in response to changed circumstances, and part of those circumstances could be the very economic analysis that is attempting to elucidate the situation. There is little doubt, for example, that trade union negotiators have changed their bargaining behaviour in the light of better information about the effects of exchange rate changes on future inflation rates, and about the effect of tax changes on take-home pay.

POLITICAL WILL

4.19 All three programmes have implicit in them some assumptions about the political will and capacity of the Government to bring about fundamental changes. For example, a monetarist programme involves reducing the power of trade unions in labour markets. It is a moot point whether the Government could get consent for legislation along these lines. Similarly, it might meet with considerable resistance to any proposal to dismantle the National Health Service. New Cambridge policy makers have been remarkably sanguine in the past about the ability of the UK to impose unilateral trade restrictions to protect UK markets. It seems quite probable that major trading nations in the EEC and beyond would retaliate by putting restrictions on UK exports. Finally, Keynesians need to consider whether other countries could be persuaded to join a global exercise to expand world demand. The onus is also on them to show how an incomes policy could be made administratively effective (and acceptable to trade unions) given the record of incomes policies in the UK in the past 15 years. It should be clear from these examples that economic policy cannot be divorced from its political context. The 'technical' solutions advocated by economists are frequently vitiated by naivety about the nature of the political process.

LONG-TERM VISION

4.20 There is however a more fundamental set of opinions implicit in these three policy alternatives. It is not difficult to argue that all three would work eventually, if they could be fully implemented given technical and political constraints. The 'eventually' indicates that the time path for any one objective (such as increasing employment) could differ markedly from one policy to another. But while the results might be the same in terms of the indicators of economic performance, the kind of society presupposed would be markedly different.

4.21 The monetarist vision is one of a free enterprise-based society with private provision of all goods and services insofar as private markets can be sensibly created. The role of the state would be sharply reduced, and its expenditure as well. Public expenditure would be met from taxation alone. The main role of the Government would be to provide an environment in which private markets could flourish. There would be an emphasis on law and order, the protection of private property rights and the legal framework for the enforcement of contracts. The welfare state would be reduced to an ultimate safety net. For most citizens social provision would be replaced by private insurance for health and unemployment, and by private saving for retirement. A vigorous anti-monopoly policy would police the behaviour of firms in private markets. Reduced taxes on income and capital, made possible by the reduction in state expenditure, would create an incentive for a small business sector that would keep large business competitive. National trade unions would disappear as major influences in the labour market and on general economic policy. Wage bargaining would take place at a local level with reference to local conditions.

4.22 The Keynesian solution implies a more corporatist vision of society. It accepts an economy dominated by large institutions, giant corporations, large trade unions, and a powerful central government. These groups are seen as having competing claims on the national economy. The objective would be to bring them into joint decision-making machinery so that the long-run behaviour of the economy could be regulated. However this would require the major institutions to be more cohesive and to have more control over their constituent parts. The ultra-Keynesianism of New Cambridge carries this view to its logical conclusion. The main groupings in the Keynesian scenario would, however, be unlikely to be able to agree on the conduct of economic policy, since their interests are conflicting. This would be 'solved' by a socialist government with its roots in the trade union movement and with substantial control, via nationalisation, of the productive sector. In both the Keynesian and the New Cambridge models, the state would also continue a large measure of involvement in social security, pensions, health and education, providing much more than a mere safety net. Equality both of outcomes and of opportunity would be as much an objective of policy as economic growth and stability.

4.23 The necessary brevity of this analysis offers something of a caricature of the nature of the options implicit in the three policy schools. But the message is that economic policy is much more than finding out 'how the economy works' and then applying the right 'instruments' to solve the perceived problems. Important though the technical analysis is, it cannot give the 'right' answer on its own. Implicit in the policy options are also profound political and ethical questions about the kind of society in which people may wish to live.

Part Two

Economic Institutions

Chapter Five

THE BUSINESS ENTERPRISE

In the first of three chapters in Part Two on economic institutions, John Pickering describes some of the influences affecting the business sector. He argues for improved performance of business generally, for a sense of stewardship and for the adoption of socially responsible policies.

5.1 So far the economic discussion has been concerned with the nature of economic theory and the method of the economist. In the next three chapters, we move the focus to consider three important economic institutions: business, work, and the state, and their impact on human behaviour. In each of these chapters we seek both to describe the nature and role of those institutions and also to identify some of the fundamental issues that need to be addressed about their role in the economy.

Business Enterprise

5.2 In large measure the creative or productive process in industrialised societies is focused in the business enterprise. The three factors of capital, workers' skills and organising ability are vital. Since the time of the industrial revolution the business enterprise has been recognised as an important engine of economic growth and wealth creation in society. Thus it is a social and economic unit of considerable importance. It provides opportunities for paid employment for many people and supplies goods and services for its customers. Out of its surpluses it allows the generation of new activities and enables society to expend resources on services provided by the public sector, which could not otherwise be financed. Through this, and through the dependence of business on the overall infrastructure, which governments and other sectors in society provide, there is considerable interdependence of business and government.

5.3 Business enterprise covers a wide variety of forms of economic activity including agriculture and mining; manufacturing; construction and the public utilities; and the service sector such as retailing, financial services, and tourism. In the past two decades the sectoral mix of economic activity in Britain has changed markedly with a decline in the share of output and employment accounted for by manufacturing, and with increasing proportionate and absolute importance being given to branches of the service sector. In addition public services, which are normally not bought or sold in the market place, but whose scale is the consequence of governmental decision, have increased their overall share of economic activity. Even within sectors, there is a continual process of change in which some industries increase in relative importance while others decline.

5.4 In Britain, as in many other economies, business organisations operate in a market economy in which the price mechanism plays a key role in influencing the allocation of resources between alternative uses. This relates closely to the operation of the profit motive since the reward for a more effective performance in identifying and satisfying consumer needs will be an increase in the profitability of the business. This may be contrasted with the use, to a greater or lesser degree, of central planning of output and investment in socialist economies.

SMALL FIRMS

5.5 In Britain at the present time there is a wide diversity in the size of businesses, ranging from a considerable number of extremely small firms (even in manufacturing industry) to a small number of very large firms accounting for a high proportion of total employment and output. This is shown in the table below. It is important not to lose sight of the economic importance of small firms. Indeed, the share of small firms in overall economic activity is even greater in some other industrialised countries and may become of increasing significance here too as a result of such developments as enterprise zones and science parks, new techniques such as microprocessors, tax changes favouring small businesses, and the incidence of management and worker buy-outs.

EMPLOYMENT IN ALL MANUFACTURING INDUSTRIES 1980

Size of enterprise by total number employed	*Enterprises*		*Establishments*		*Employment*	
	No.	*%*	*No.*	*%*	*No. '000*	*%*
1–99	84,944	94.21	89,230	82.24	1,145.7	18.77
100–999	4,515	5,01	9,061	8.35	1,213.7	19.89
1,000–4,999	548	0.61	4,597	4.24	1,123.9	18.41
5,000–9,999	79	0.09	1,962	1.81	550.4	9.02
10,000–49,999	69	0.08	2,832	2.62	1,348.3	22.09
50,000 and over	8	0.01	816	0.75	721.5	11.82
Total	90.163	100	108,498	100	6,103.5	100

Source: Business Statistics Office *Report on the Census of Production 1980* PA1002 Summary Tables, Table 12, HMSO 1983

(Note: this table excludes energy industries and public sector enterprises)

LARGE FIRMS

5.6 However, when focusing on modern business enterprise, most people will think particularly of 'big business': the large, diversified company with many different products and activities, often having production operations in a number of overseas countries and with a complex management and control system. Some companies are indeed so large that the value of their annual sales exceeds the GNP of certain nation states. Their significance in the economy and the implications of their ability to move production operations around the globe may be such that they are sometimes thought to be able to exercise undue economic and political influence. While some of these organisations may still be substantially under the control of the families of their founders and others may be owned by the state, the vast majority are publicly quoted companies in which there is a separation of ownership from control. Here too there has been a fundamental change in the pattern of ownership with a decline in the proportion of shares held by private individuals and an increase in the proportion held by institutional investors, such as insurance companies and pension funds.

CHANGE AND CONCENTRATION

5.7 Business organisations do not stand still. They are under continual pressure from competition in markets, from the ebb and flow of demand for particular products, from the effects of economic fluctuations and uncertainty, and from management and shareholders seeking growth and performance improvements. In many industries, emphasis will be placed upon maintaining a high utilisation of productive capacity since without this costs will rise and profits fall. Firms will therefore seek as much stability and predictability in their markets as they can achieve. In this they may look to the Government for help through its demand management policies or its role as a customer. In other cases, emphasis may be put on marketing activities (such as advertising or special promotions) to try to achieve the level of sales required to clear planned output. There will often be an emphasis on developing new products to replace older ones and this will point to the need for various forms of research, design and development work. This is now particularly expensive (relative to the number of new products launched) in some industries such as, for example, the pharmaceuticals industry.

5.8 Given the large size of many firms it is less possible for a significant number to co-exist in any particular product market. Thus the number of alternative suppliers may well be limited, although consumer choice may be wider due to the proliferation of brands from individual suppliers. Increasingly, the typical market structure is one with a few suppliers recognising their mutual interdependence in the market. They respond, not so much to the operation of impersonal market forces, as to the actions of the other major firms in their industry. Thus competition becomes more direct between the individual firms concerned and involves the development of strategies having their effect in markets throughout the global area covered by these firms. This tendency to concentration of sources of supply in a market is also to some extent mirrored in a concentration of purchasing power by industrial companies and, in the context of consumer products, by the increasingly important retail chains.

The Growth of Big Business

5.9 While there are countervailing trends encouraging the development of small firms, big business has become particularly important. There are three general types of explanation for this.

ECONOMIES OF SCALE

5.10 For any process of production (whether of goods or services), given the state of technology, there is likely to be an optimal scale of plant and hence of output. It is often argued that in order to reap the full benefit (through lower unit costs) of technical progress there is a need for larger units. However, this does not explain the growth of larger firms, owning many separate plants, often in quite disparate areas of economic activity. There are also economies of scale in the process of research and development or in marketing and distribution, that encourage such trends. In addition, firms derive benefits from their overall size in their ability to use a stronger asset base to take on larger projects or orders, to raise capital more cheaply, to spread risks and to even out the flows of profits through diversification.

MANAGEMENT

5.11 Given developments in management methods and control procedures, large organisations may be able to manage their activities more efficiently and expand more successfully the range of activities with which individual managers can be involved. Managements may seek the growth of the business in order to broaden their own range of responsibility (and hence their prospective earning power). It is also not unknown for firms to seek to expand, perhaps by acquiring other firms, in order to increase their protection from competitive pressures.

SOCIAL AND POLITICAL INFLUENCES

5.12 Different social influences are also at work in encouraging the growth of big business. Shareholders and financial institutions generally emphasise this by their behaviour in buying and selling shares and hence in influencing the stock market rating given to acquisition-oriented companies. Governments may also influence this by encouraging mergers (believing in the advantage of larger units) or through elements of fiscal policy or company law which may favour large firms at the expense of small.

Poor Performance in Britain

5.13 The world economy in general has been suffering recently from severe recession, though as chapter three has emphasised there are also long-term changes in progress as well. Unemployment rates have risen markedly in the past 10–15 years in almost all industrialised countries. However the British problem appears in some respects to be worse than average since Britain's share of world manufacturing output and of world trade has declined faster than that of other countries, its historic rate of economic growth has been low and company profitability has also been low.

5.14 The reasons for this relatively poor performance by the UK are complex. There is no single explanation and many alternative views have been expressed, some of which necessarily extend beyond the specifically economic into wider human and political considerations. The next four paragraphs indicate those factors which seem, at least to this writer, to have a particular significance.

LACK OF DYNAMISM

5.15 There has been an undue concentration within the British economy on those industries that have experienced the greatest decline in demand or have suffered most from competition from overseas producers. Many companies have been slow to adopt new technology and, hence, to move into new activities. The productivity of both labour and of new capital investment has been lower here than in many other industrial countries. Products supplied by British companies have too often been unsophisticated and do not reflect the more specialised demands of customers with rising incomes. Too little serious commitment has been made to gaining export markets. The growth in concentration through mergers has also not been matched by increased performance and there is a general lack of competition and dynamism within much of the industrial sector.

MANAGERIAL FACTORS

5.16 The quality of industrial management has not always been up to the demands placed upon it. Managers have not had the confidence to manage positively and to invest in new capacity. Difficult industrial relations have not helped the situation, though the problem has been more about unofficial and sudden stoppages than about long-drawn-out official strikes. Unfortunately the latter have been publicised abroad and this has harmed the British reputation for reliability and delivery on time. Business enterprise generally appears to have a lower social status in Britain than elsewhere, and the profit motive has been misunderstood and sometimes despised. This again has weakened public confidence in, and commitment to, a viable business sector.

THE FORM OF CORPORATE GROWTH

5.17 Much of the growth in influence of big business over the past 25 years or so and the increase in industrial concentration (both within individual industries and in the economy as a whole) has come about as a result of mergers and acquisitions rather than through the internal growth of more efficient companies. Such mergers are often demanding of substantial managerial and other resources if they are to be effective. Research evidence tends to suggest that on balance such mergers have not been conducive to increased economic efficiency and they may reduce competition within industries. This may well have impaired overall industrial performance in Britain.

THE INFLUENCE OF THE PUBLIC SECTOR

5.18 The influence of the public sector has made profitable and dynamic business difficult. This is due to instability in the macroeconomic environment caused by fluctuations in government policy, often adopted with a counter-cyclical purpose in mind to try to offer greater economic stability! The overall difficulties imposed on companies of all sizes by the general weight of public administration in terms of the need for form filling and negotiations with central and local government, etc., also tend to deflect from the more creative role of business. The quality of such administration has sometimes been criticised, but it has also been held that the high calibre of personnel recruited into the public service has tended to reduce to an undesirable extent the pool of able people available to work in the wealth creating sectors of the economy.

Issues for the Future

5.19 The future prospects for businesses of all sizes and in all activities, at least for the next few years, seem likely to be fraught with considerable changes and uncertainties. The introduction of new technologies will involve new ways of doing things and further shifts in the nature of employment opportunities. From new technologies and other developments will come changes in the pattern of demand. The severity of international competition will continue to increase in many markets. In the British context questions will continue to be asked about the extent to which manufacturing industries should be preserved or whether service industries can produce an increasing share of the desired real income for the economy as a whole. The form and extent of state intervention in industrial development will be an important issue. Thus business will have to face a wide range of practical and ethical issues arising both from its continuing activities and from the rapid process of transformation which it is experiencing.

5.20 Any attempt to offer prescriptions for the future requires clarification of the ethical basis, or value system, which underpins the proposals. The starting point adopted here assumes that the profit motive is an acceptable mechanism since profit is a return to entrepreneurial skill and investment. However this is only acceptable as long as it is bounded by competitive market pressures (or by external constraints where markets do not exercise adequate controls) and directed by a sense of responsibility and stewardship on the part of decision-takers who would seek to order affairs in ways consistent with Christian standards of justice and equity, concern for others and accountability.

RAISING PERFORMANCE

5.21 Some alleviation of the British problems could be sought by action to raise economic performance in the business sector generally. (To the extent that this increased overall efficiency and led to rising real incomes this need not be at the expense of suppliers elsewhere.) Steps to overcome the difficulties identified in paragraphs 5.15–5.17 would probably feature strongly in any set of prescriptions. However, while technical economic responses are, of course, important, the wider contribution from increased attention to the human aspects of business, involving both employees and customers, is also important. The nature of the response will vary from case to case. In some the opportunity for greater participation by employees in aspects of decision taking or in the rewards from the performance of the company may be appropriate. In many it seems likely that improved human relations and better understanding of each other's needs and aspirations may be the key.

5.22 A particular aspect of this concerns the question of organisation structure. Whereas in the small company there is likely to be close rapport between owners, managers (who may be the same people), employees and often customers too, in the larger organisation this is less likely to be found. Indeed in some cases the ultimate point of control and authority is removed from the vision of individual workers who may not even know the identity of the parent company for whom they are ultimately working. A more decentralised organisation structure may encourage greater identification with and commitment to the success of the organisation, with beneficial effects to both employees and corporate performance. The recent growth of management buy-outs is another means whereby this is being accomplished.

STEWARDSHIP

5.23 It is a feature of much modern business that responsibility for the use of considerable resources is vested in a limited number of people. The need for effective and responsible stewardship of these resources and the opportunities they create should be apparent. Large companies may have scope for the exercise of considerable economic power, though competition between large firms (which may be severe), government controls and consumer pressures may restrict this power. Companies will need to consider the extent to which socially responsible policies should be adopted even if they lessen the profitability of the enterprise (though this is not always the inevitable outcome). Aspects of companies' pricing and marketing decisions, employment and personnel policies, attitudes to the use of depletable resources, etc., may need to come under ethical scrutiny. In the case of transnational companies operating in overseas countries, especially developing countries where their global power may give them particular leverage over the host country, these issues may be especially important.

5.24 The influence of conglomerates–widely diversified companies–is something which merits consideration. As companies broaden their range of activities and have scope to transfer profits from one line of business to another, so investors, employees and consumers may find themselves wondering whether by patronising that particular organisation they are in fact helping to foster other activities (e.g. gambling, brewing, cigarettes, etc.) with which they may prefer not to be associated. There is a further potential problem with conglomerates where the possibility arises of less than full disclosure of the performance of individual business units within the company. This makes it difficult for others to see precisely where profits are being earned. Not only may this be harmful to overall economic efficiency, it also does not assist the investor who seeks to handle his funds responsibly. Attention should therefore be given to the possibility of greater disclosure of information about such large companies.

5.25 An important feature of the British scene in recent years has been the growing importance of financial institutions, such as banks, insurance companies and pension funds, as providers of investment finance and as shareholders in major companies. They have an important stewardship role to exercise. There are two aspects of this which sometimes give rise to expressions of concern. First, it is argued that the financial institutions tend to have a more short-term, risk-averse, approach to corporate finance than the development of business really requires. Secondly, it is a matter for concern that stockmarkets sometimes appear to be more concerned with short-term financial gains through takeover booms and asset stripping than with a long-term commitment to the production of goods and services in the 'real' economy.

5.26 If the British economic system is to be built in large measure around the assumption of competitively working markets, it is important that markets should actually work in the way that is required of them–rewarding the efficient, preventing abuses of monopoly power, encouraging a responsible use of resources. While business may help through its own sense of social responsibility and through voluntary Codes of Practice, an effective competition policy has a key role to play. Britain has several agencies in this field such as the Office of Fair Trading, the Monopolies and Mergers Commission and the Restrictive Trade Practices Court. There are various pieces of legislation seeking to promote competition and enhance consumer protection in the public interest and the EEC has its own system of competition policy. A vigorous and consistent application of competition policy is a key contributor to effectively operating markets.

THE PROCESS OF ADJUSTMENT

5.27 Where a process of change is taking place for which the underlying economic forces are strong, it is difficult to resist the trend. Indeed, in economic terms it may be inefficient and wasteful of resources in a general equilibrium sense to attempt to do so. This does not, however, mean that all change is easy to accommodate. Where it is of a radical nature and accompanied by recession and increasing international competition the effects are especially severe. It should be noted that such changes do not necessarily point to the inevitability of larger companies and less employment. In some instances this may be the outcome, and positive responses will be required to mitigate the adverse economic effects on those directly affected. In others, new technologies will create new jobs and may make it possible for small businesses to compete more effectively against larger companies. Indeed, it may be that positive adjustment policies may be desirable, actively working with the process of change but providing help in the form of retraining, mobility grants, access to risk capital, etc., for those who are harmed by the changes.

5.28 One, perhaps natural, tendency in times of economic turbulence such as we are currently experiencing is to call for increased protection from the rigours of competition. Various forms of short-term protection through cartels and import restrictions are sometimes advocated and used to help a process of industrial adjustment. However their effects and method of operation require very careful scrutiny since they deny to consumers the opportunity to buy at more competitive prices and weaken the impact of market processes on the efficiency of the companies concerned. Of even greater importance though is the effect which protectionism has on producers in less developed countries who are thereby denied the opportunity to sell their products in the often larger and more wealthy markets of industrialised countries. Thus calls for protectionism should raise particular doubts in the minds of those who are concerned for a Christian ethic in business. However, controls on 'dumping', where the effect is to disturb a market by selling at prices which do not reflect long-run costs of supply, may be more justifiable.

5.29 If the effect of the availability of new technologies is to allow a transfer from labour-intensive to capital-intensive methods of production, it is likely, and should indeed be expected, that those businesses that are part of this process should be generating considerable surpluses or profits. While some of these profits will be required to sustain and develop the immediate business, it is important that some will be recycled to create employment opportunities for others. These may be through other manufacturing operations, through service activities in the private sector or through programmes of social provision and improvement to amenities throughout the country. A positive and creative role for business, recognising the resources and opportunities entrusted to its stewardship, has perhaps never been so important.

Chapter Six
THE COMMUNITY OF WORK

In the second of three chapters in Part Two on economic institutions, John Hughes argues that, in the current economic situation, trade unions need to transcend narrow vested interests. As they have sought to redistribute income and resources, so they are now called upon to redistribute work itself and to take a greater share in the responsibilities of ownership through shared control of pension funds.

Tensions at Work

6.1 It is increasingly evident that major changes are sweeping over the world of work as it affects, not just business and government, but employees as well and the communities in which they live. In Britain and in many European countries large-scale structural unemployment is now challenging the economic fabric of society and its moral calibre.

6.2 Conventional commercial accountancy treats paid work as a *cost* to business, as a commodity. The practical tensions, however, surrounding paid work in modern, commercialised economies cannot be so easily glossed over. For such work may be seen as a cost by the worker, as an imposed and burdensome rhythm, but it also represents a personal need. It is the assumed foundation of most social organisation and plays a critical part in personal development and identity. Worker and employer may both treat wage work as a cost, but they mean profoundly different things by it. They may differ still more as to whether workers are mere *means* within an economic process directed (and possibly withdrawn) by others.

6.3 Alongside the evolution of industrial and commercial society has gone the widening collective organisation and combination of workers. The development of combined action in order to represent the concerns of people in their working lives, has modified in important ways the management of economic resources and the evolution of political and social democracy. Workers' interests challenge and transcend both the material interests of profit-orientated production and state-directed identification of social needs. The potentialities of communities of workers in directing (and redirecting) the use of resources are not without significance. Representative reponsibilities in face of the changing character of employment, and trusteeship over organisational practice, are not static and routine matters, least of all when large capital resources (as with pension funds), or human resources (as with trade union membership) are concerned.

UNEMPLOYMENT

6.4 Paid work in many countries, and not least in Britain, is subject to all the aspects of dynamic change and unresolved crisis. Thus in the UK in three recent years over two million jobs have disappeared, and the 'jobs gap' (the difference between the existing number of jobs and the number of people who would be seeking work under previously experienced economic conditions) has climbed towards four million. Most of the lost jobs were in full-time manual work, chiefly in manufacturing, and most of the unemployed are thus manual workers. There is now across the UK one unemployed manual worker for every four still in full-time manual employment. There are also four times as many unemployed under the age of 25 as the entire strength of the country's armed forces.

6.5 The critical tensions of work and wages are not just a matter of temporary unemployment thrown up by a short-lived recession. Across much of Europe analysts expect current levels of unemployment to persist or to worsen. In Britain longer-term unemployment has greatly increased. Between the end of 1980 and the end of 1983 the underlying increase in the number unemployed for over one year was nearly fourfold. A major change in the organisation of work and a new dimension of sharing and participation in economic life is now seen, for example, by the European Commission and other agencies, as necessary and as requiring an internationally co-ordinated approach.

INEQUALITIES

6.6 This does not mean that the problems are only those of lack of employment. The crisis of values and responsibility within the area of existing employment continues to be unresolved. There are deep-seated problems, for example, in achieving felt fairness in the conditions, responsibilities and rewards of work, particular as they concern the low paid or workers in public services. There are inequalities in the distribution of work (such as excessive hours and a protracted working life for some alongside considerable structural unemployment for others, or inferior status, rights and opportunities for part-time workers in comparison with those who have full-time jobs). The old category of *full-time* work looks all too rigid compared, for example, with the needs of young workers for movement and discovery, or of older workers for recuperation and an adjustment to interests outside work, or the needs of women with extensive family responsibilities.

6.7 Many kinds of inequality in work persist. There are still important elements of differentiation between non-manual work (now representing the majority of jobs in the UK economy) and manual work with regard to working time, income security and career opportunities. Attempts to remove these and other forms of discrimination (for example, against women workers) are still resisted. Besides this, new technology is signalling its displacement of many existing kinds of work. Consequently it becomes increasingly urgent that people should have the educational and social skills to adapt to new tasks. Working time and working lives need to be organised with continuing links with education and training to enhance such adaptability. The challenge to our social, political and economic institutions is not only to initiate new work in place of the old, but also to share and re-organise work and working life, and to offer more access to creative personal and social activity outside the time occupied by paid work.

6.8 The capacity of people to organise themselves constructively to meet these challenges is important in modern economies, for the large-scale commercial enterprise operating under international competitive pressure is likely to continue to view its labour requirements as 'costs' to be minimised. At the same time the state is caught up in the dilemma of meeting multiple social and individual needs out of constrained revenue. It is unlikely that either of these great agencies of economic organisation will be able to respond sufficiently to meet the needs, or to make full use of the resources, of working people and their communities.

TRADE UNIONS

6.9 Trade union organisation to represent workers' interests is virtually as widespread as the wage system itself. In the UK, recent years have seen a rise in the proportion of employees who are union members (from around 50 per cent a decade ago to some 60 per cent by the early 1980s), and unionisation is particularly high in the larger plants and enterprises and in public sector services and industries. Most of this membership is concentrated in large trade unions (four-fifths of the total, in the 25 unions with membership over 100,000). Many of these trade unions are structured like business conglomerates with membership interests ranging across a number of sectors or occupations. This has come about because trade unions have developed in response to the commodity status of labour and are operating in the labour market. In trade unions, as in business firms, survival and effectiveness depends on the combined resources of many groups, on crossing old frontiers as industries and technologies change and develop. There have been material, self-interested, reasons, therefore, why trade unionism has moved on beyond a relatively narrow identification with the sectional interests of specific groups of working people, towards a wider solidarity. But trade union organisational links have also widened out to reach from workplace groups to international federations and, in contrast to business, these links are handled through a range of representative and democratic processes.

6.10 Many conflicting and competing interests, however, between different groups and organisations of workers persist. Trade unions spend much of their time and energy seeking to reconcile and harmonise these pluralist interests and to establish and express a wider solidarity. Trade unions are *from* and *in* the competitive commercial economy, but they can also begin to transcend it.

6.11 These responsibilities in face of competing interests and unresolved issues of pay differentials are greatly increased in the contemporary economy. The apparent completeness of trade union concern for workers and for the representation of working people that sprang from a fully-employed economy looks very different in face of large-scale structural unemployment. Trade unions need in practice to transcend narrow vested interests. But it is still unclear whether they will in the main express the short-run sectional interests of workers currently *in work* or whether they will be able to advance the interests of *all workers* and above all those most disadvantaged, the unemployed. Unemployment is, after all, the least defensible differential of all. Trade unionism has sought to redistribute and share income and resources; now it is called upon to redistribute and share work itself.

INDUSTRIAL RELATIONS

6.12 Trade unions in the UK have not been helped to develop a more forward looking and socially responsible role in recent years. They have been substantially shut out of any major involvement in the planning and deployment of resources for development, both in enterprises and in public services. In the private sector such development has been widely resisted by business. In addition, in their traditional collective bargaining British trade unions have been from the mid 1960s (and in the name of incomes policies) pushed back from longer-term agreements into short-run, one year, agreements on pay and conditions. Such short time horizons for bargaining do not help the forward-looking re-organisation of work and its rewards that the processes of economic change have clearly put on the agenda. In these and other ways the industrial relations practices in the UK have been, and are, ill-designed to produce socially constructive outcomes. Exaggerated claims for free collective bargaining that have developed under these conditions can be contrasted with the inadequate reality. The word 'free' has appeared a question-begging one to many workers under the pressure of threatened and actual closures and redundancy.

6.13 Britain, then, has something to learn from Continental systems of industrial relations that involve a greater sharing of control over longer-term development in enterprises and in public services and in the improvement of labour skills and education. This would involve a profound shift of trade union organisation, responsibilities and functions. It would also be a challenge to the more authoritarian styles of management, both private and public. It is not a matter of asking for industrial peace within the present structure of authority, but of working for a response that handles power and resources more constructively, with more concern to renew economic activity for those who have been discarded from, or denied entry to, paid work.

6.14 There are not only large institutions of organised labour, but also large numbers of individuals who take on responsibilities for representing their fellow workers, and working voluntarily to meet their needs, within the structures of trade unionism. The many linkages of the trade union movement enable this to be for many a widening learning experience. That learning is, in part, about democratic processes and the awkward realities of economic factors. It is also an experience of moral challenge, and of fresh consideration as to who is my neighbour, as wider responsibilities and the reconciliation of interests, have to be faced. Trade unions stand as a countervailing power to that of business enterprise, a reminder that labour in the economy is more than a cost. The negative force that this can represent is clear, but the constructive role of social labour has still not been fully explored.

A New Ownership Role

6.15 One example of the contemporary challenge to trustee responsibilities, and to the old categories of labour and capital, comes from the greatly enlarged scope of pension funds, particularly in the UK and the USA. Typically both enterprises and employees contribute to them, and their objective is to provide funds for employees' pensions. To the employer they are part of current labour costs, but they are also a commitment for the future. To workers they are workers' capital funds (trade unions would say deferred pay). The traditional stance has been to build up and hold a spread of financial investments to meet long-term calls on the fund. With post-war inflation has come a shift to a larger holding of real assets such as property. There has also been a major switch to risk-bearing (and potentially controlling) equity shares in companies. The traditional stance assumed a passive role, as ownership of shares and holdings was spread rather than concentrated. If questions were raised about the performance or prospects of any company the response would be to sell, rather than to use ownership rights in order to challenge or to seek change.

6.16 But these acorns have grown into oaks. For more than a generation private holders of shares have been selling to financial institutions (insurance companies as well as pension funds) until, considered collectively, the institutions have become a dominant force in the ownership of the equity of UK companies. In both Britain and the USA pension funds hold around a quarter of all the equity of the quoted companies in those countries. This dominance grows as investments are built up through the sums that accrue to such funds each year (currently, in Britain, an additional £15,000 million a year, split almost equally between pension funds and insurance companies). The biggest pension funds and insurance companies now have large holdings in the companies that set the pace for the economy. This has profoundly altered the nature of the 'private' ownership of industry. The funds have in this sense been termed the 'absentee landlords of the industrial estate'. Despite the scale of individual funds and of institutional holdings, most of them still operate without active intervention in the enterprises in which, taken together, they nominally have a controlling share.

TRUSTEE RESPONSIBILITIES

6.17 The implied challenge to the nature of trustee responsibilities in such funds cannot be in doubt. Few funds have begun to share the process of managerial control with trustees representative of employees and pensioners, and few such trustees have been equipped for these responsibilities. But the fact of the continuing crisis of UK economic development and the massive flow of savings into institutions for investment for the long-run pension needs of employees, provides an unmistakable challenge. The contrast between the loss of over two million jobs in the UK in three years and the potential for assisting business development that resides in these funds (which absorb the savings of over ten million workers) should encourage new and more active thinking about investment and ownership responsibilities.

6.18 But the old stance is changing, albeit slowly. Larger funds have learned how to share the risks of new commercial development in smaller companies. Through consortia they share their financial resources, and their access to expertise, in a more actively engaged form of ownership. This is now beginning to be translated also into a more challenging role in larger enterprises (the institutional take-over of Woolworths being a substantial straw in the wind). Joint initiatives, a more persistent development of the whole range of managerial and entrepreneurial skills, and less stress on the autonomy of each fund, are needed for a more active and longer-run view of ownership to develop. Just as the individual non-unionised worker may react to bad management by leaving, while the collectively organised group stays and tries to improve its conditions through collective action, so the pension funds should shed their traditional stance of walking away from economic problems (by selling) and stay to act together to improve performance and prospects.

6.19 Nor is this only a matter of financial returns and the UK economy. In what may be straightforwardly seen as workers' funds, trusteeship–exercised through ownership rights–must ask whether management is treating workers fairly as well as efficiently. Such concerns stretch round the globe, given the transnational character of most large enterprises. They may not be resolved by walking away (selling) where exploitation and discrimination are issues, but by combining the resources of such trusteeship to change policy. The moral challenge stemming from the thought that millions of workers are in the sense outlined here, the most important and growing force in the 'private ownership' of industry and commerce will not go away.

6.20 It is unlikely ever to be an easy process for those representing workers' interests to seek to take a wider view of their responsibilities. Yet some at least of the traditions of organised labour emphasise a wider solidarity, and a more extensive community of interests. In the aftermath of structural change and crisis in Britain, the tension between the priority to be given to the interests of those in employment as against the unemployed is a particularly difficult matter to handle. This is not simply a matter of the morality of trade union practice. Neither the state nor major employers have yet done much to open up constructively new moral worlds, new choices and opportunities, for organised labour. Vigorous resistance to reduced working time has been more evident than a socially constructive effort to create and share job opportunities. There has been quite as widespread a resistance by business and by public authorities to any sharing of power and responsibility as to the resources and priorities involved in the development of enterprises and public services. Trade unions have to be asked to use social power constructively but so too do the other institutions with power and initiative in the 'labour market'.

Chapter Seven
THE STATE

In the last of three chapters in Part Two on economic institutions, John Hughes argues for a new balance of commercial energy and social well-being. He outlines a role for the state in enabling resources, which may be employed or unemployed at the moment, to be directed into economically constructive channels.

A Mixed Economy

7.1 This third chapter in Part Two considers the economics of the nation state and the constraints and opportunities which face it in the management of the economy. Britain has what is termed a mixed economy and the phrase recognises the very substantial direct role the state plays in its economic life. This embraces spending by public authorities, on goods and services (such as social services and defence) and on transfer payments (such as benefits). One way of measuring the progress of such public expenditure is to express it as a proportion of gross domestic product (GDP), that is, the total output of the country's goods and services. For the UK, as for existing members of the European Community generally, the ratio of public expenditure to GDP has risen from just under a third in 1960 to just under a half in recent years. The table below shows this in more detail.

PUBLIC EXPENDITURE AS A PROPORTION OF GDP 1960–1980

Year	*UK*	*All European Community members*
1960	32.6	31.8
1970	42.0	37.4
1975	47.7	45.7
1980	43.9	46.5

Source: *European Economy* July 1981

7.2 But the term mixed economy embraces more than a direct concern with public spending. It recognises too the wider influence of the state. This is partly concerned with economic relations with other countries internationally and the ways in which policies (for example towards protectionism or changes in currency exchange rates) affect international trade. This aspect of the activity of the state is, in Europe particularly, developing through the increased inter-dependence of the major economies. The wider influence of the state in the mixed economy has also developed internally through the scale and structure of taxation, and through direct and indirect influence on the conduct of business, of finance and of labour markets (including pay policies).

REAPPRAISAL

7.3 Currently, the economic role of the state in many mixed economies is under reappraisal and more difficulties are perceived, and more disagreements encountered, than in earlier post-war decades. In place of the comparatively easy growth of economies characteristic of the 1950s and 1960s the decade since 1973 has in Europe been characterised by slow and erratic growth. For particular countries and sectors, such as the UK and its manufacturing industries, more acute problems of national economic development have emerged and have not been resolved. Consequently, many mixed economies have been unable to ensure full employment, and this has thrown more strain in turn on the social welfare policies earlier pursued. While economic growth was sustained and tax revenues were buoyant, there was less difficulty, politically as well as economically, in combining improvements in social welfare with the incentives and drives of commerce. There is now a striking contrast between the social and economic needs to be met across much of Europe and the extent to which resources, both human and capital, are either unemployed or under-employed.

7.4 In face of such troubles it is not surprising that contemporary governments are being urged from many sides to take major initiatives in the handling of their economies. Nor is it surprising if conflicting advice is offered, or conflicting demands are presented by different social and economic groups. We have already made it clear that some of these disagreements arise from the various schools of economic analysis. But uncertainty about the longer-run consequences for the economy of particular policies and actions also arises from other causes. The state is confronted with structural changes in market competitiveness and growth, in new technologies, and in labour markets and the skills required in them. This calls for the redirection of the use of resources within the public sector, in the balance of responsibilities between both public and private enterprise and in the kinds of initiatives sought, or stimulated, in industrial and commercial business.

PARTNERSHIP

7.5 With many parts of the economic system facing a difficult period of transition in organisation, function, adaptation of existing skills, coupled with the social urgency generated by the displacement of large numbers of workers from paid employment, the state needs to work with the other agencies that command, or influence, the use of material and human resources. It can assist others to cope with the structural changes and adjustment problems that are part of the difficult path to new development. It is not a period for the state to abandon its responsibilities within the national community, nor in wider economic communities internationally. Neither is it one in which the state should act as if it could monopolise economic responsibilities. What is needed instead is a *sharing* of resources and risks. The critical problems of economic development, of the search for a new balance of commercial energy and social well-being, are not likely to be resolved by an undue emphasis on the sovereign and coercive power of the state in economic life, nor on its unilateral authority. But the state can join in initiatives, and enable resources, employed and unemployed at the moment, to be redirected into economically constructive channels.

7.6 In this sense many of the constraints on the ability of the state to resolve the crises of development and decline are to be seen as opportunities. International inter-dependence, for example, means that it is more difficult for an individual country to pursue its own development regardless of the impact its choice of policies may have on its neighbours. But that challenge, once recognised, should provoke the response of shared and mutually supportive initiatives. If neither the state nor business *alone* can carry the burden of providing for the nation's economic development, then the need and opportunity arises for a new social and economic dialogue about the shared responsibilities of what are known elsewhere as 'social partners' (industrial and commercial businesses, financial institutions, workers and their representatives) in enabling development to proceed effectively.

Within the Public Sector

7.7 With this in mind, it is helpful to review the main ways in which the state's social and economic services and organisations function. We proceed in turn from those state functions most dominated by criteria of individual or social need to those which combine elements of response to social need with 'market' economics.

BENEFITS

7.8 One modification of the market economy is the provision of state benefits to the dependent population. Some of this may be viewed primarily as 'compulsory insurance' which redistributes income over people's lifetimes. Much of it (such as child benefits), however, represents an important element of the social *transfer* of income. In the complex system in Britain acute strains have developed in this system, stemming from the failure of contribution-based National Insurance Benefits to provide adequate levels of income support as a right. With the increase in unemployment and the growth of new patterns of need (one million single parent families, for example), a substantial increase has taken place in the number of people claiming supplementary benefit (4.3 million in 1982). Over 6 million people are now estimated to be living on supplementary benefit, or at even lower levels of income, though the DHSS *Social Security Statistics 1982* indicates that only 70 per cent of potential claimants actually receive supplementary benefit. Other means-tested benefits have also increased and, at the same time, income tax at the full standard rate and National Insurance contributions are levied on people earning well below average incomes. As a result problems have been created for numbers of households. If they raise their low income, for example, the overlap of income tax and the withdrawal of means-tested benefits can have the effect of almost totally removing the extra they have earned. *The Third Report of the House of Commons Treasury and Civil Service Committee May 1983* estimated that, for 1980, 500,000 poor working families, with around 1½ million people in them, faced effective tax rates on additional income of 60 per cent or more. (By contrast only 70,000 high tax-payers faced a rate of 60 per cent or more on their incomes.) Recent Government evidence to this Committee has also pointed out that (in April 1982) a married couple with two children could face a theoretical tax rate of more than 100 per cent over the income ranged from £47 to £82 a week. A near doubling of gross earnings could mean a reduction in net income. This 'poverty trap', as it is called, together with growing numbers needing supplementary benefit, are signs of increasing social stress as the economy comes under strain from loss of economic growth, while government seeks to curb the growing cost of social security. They indicate too that the principles of equity and of respect for those in need are all too imperfectly observed.

PUBLIC SERVICES

7.9 There has been in Britain a widespread acceptance of public responsibility for the provision of a range of services based on social need rather than ability to pay, such as defence, health, education and environmental services. Social need is not itself a static or agreed foundation, and re-interpretation of priorities in the fulfilment of need is an essential element of public debate and democratic policy making. But it is clear also that respect for social need has by no means replaced 'ability to pay' in the total provision of such services. If financial pressures on the state lead to constrained and inadequate public 'needs-based' services, a market sector of commercially provided services is likely to develop (e.g. in education and in health). This may also have the effect of creating difficult issues of social values, double standards and inequality.

7.10 The desire for a more adequate response to structural shifts in the economy is putting important questions on the agenda as to the social priorities of the public services. Fresh debate is also emerging about the efficiency and accountability of these services, and about the mix of national government, local government and local community responsibility. It is worth remembering that the public is the employer of some five million people in this sector, that much of the cost is for labour, and that standards of fair comparison and efficiency have not been universally agreed in the past and are matters of continuing controversy.

7.11 As with state benefits and income transfers, collectively provided services constitute a large segment of the economy. The social quality and social values of British society are particularly expressed in these sectors. The required responses are not self-evident and are unlikely to be costless, as the country re-thinks the ways in which it should meet both individual and collective needs in a changing social and economic system.

PUBLIC UTILITIES

7.12 In major sectors of the economy, and particularly in transport, energy, communications, housing and water supply, public corporations combine social need with more strictly commercial practices. In a number of cases effective monopoly provision (for example, water supply) has been seen as the most efficient way of creating an integrated supply system providing an adequate service for the maximum possible number of consumers. Provision for holding these agencies accountable and the public determination of guidelines for their financial objectives, have been viewed as ways of avoiding both the abuse of such monopoly power and excessive reliance on the public purse to subsidise particular activities. In some cases there is, in practice, competition with private sector suppliers (for example, oil in the energy sector) and wider issues of commercial fairness intrude.

7.13 Most recently telecommunications have gained in economic significance owing to the importance and future potential of rapidly advancing technology and is at the same time a matter of social concern. If the next stages of technology, for example, enable two-way audio-visual conferences for groups in different locations, this will have interesting implications for business practice and could also transform the style of and potential for democratic participation in a range of organisations. Again the old assumption of static organisational structures is giving way to new patterns of organisation and changing objectives. There is also a further concern about licensing arrangements and rules of conduct for agencies and firms operating in this rapidly developing telecommunications network. As argued earlier, it is not a matter of the state monopolising the whole area or withdrawing from it, it is a matter of a wider sharing of responsibility, in the context of democratic debate and increased openness, for the shaping of the future of society.

PUBLIC ENTERPRISES

7.14 We distinguish between 'utilities' and other 'public enterprises' because the latter work in a world of competition much of which is international.

7.15 There has been until very recently an increase in public ownership because the commercial risks and the levels of financial support and capital expenditure required could not be, or were unlikely to be, accepted by private commercial enterprise (such as in the case of steel, shipbuilding, Rolls-Royce and BL). In some cases the use of public ownership to 'rescue' firms and industries was directly connected with the wish to sustain the large net export surplus previously generated. To allow such enterprises to collapse would have greatly intensified the problems of the UK's balance of payments and made it far more difficult to pay for necessary imports and to continue the growth of the economy. In addition collapse would in some cases (Rolls-Royce, Ferranti) have meant the loss of extremely important groups able to handle highly advanced technology. In other cases it would have greatly increased unemployment and sent wider shock-waves through the economy as suppliers and others faced the collapse of their order-books. This is what happened between 1980 and 1982 when economic slump was not accompanied by any major state rescue. In manufacturing, output fell nearly 20 per cent, employment by over 20 per cent, capital investment by over 30 per cent, and the still substantial export surplus in the manufacturing sector was eliminated.

7.16 The problems of competitiveness and efficiency, however, have meant that under public ownership there has been a major task of reorganisation and rationalisation. This has been a difficult matter for public policy and finance. Sustaining and re-equipping such firms and industries (steel, BL, coal) has involved large-scale public funding. Coping with the employment and other consequences of closures and rationalisation has also involved heavy funding and severe social costs for many communities.

7.17 The country, therefore, through the state, took over the risks and responsibilities of ownership in a number of sectors in an effort to provide a longer-run basis of viability for continued commercial operation and development. It is a matter of debate whether, when such enterprises have been firmly re-established, they should then be returned to private enterprise.

But the rules applied to them should not breach the general rules of competition and company responsibility in the long-term. It would be in the community's interest if all public enterprises of this kind became models of business efficiency and responsibility, including responsible industrial relations practices. They are, however, primarily commercial in their long-term orientation.

Outside the Public Sector

7.18 Besides interacting with these sectors of the economy over which there is direct control the state also interacts with the wider economy of the UK. It has, for example, a relationship with the mass of the working population selling, or seeking to sell, its skills in the labour market. The state seeks to influence, not only the organisational behaviour of business but also the attitudes and organisational concerns of labour. An increasingly important part of this is the provision made for the continuing education and training of workers (for the development and up-dating of vocational skills and for constructive and informed participation in the management of business concerns both public and private). There has been an extension of trustee responsibilities in, for example, financial institutions such as pension funds, and the majority of workers, as members of such funds are now jointly involved in the ownership of substantial capital assets. The state will be increasingly interested in the accountability of such agencies to their members, and concerned to support the constructive, long-term, role of such investment in the future development of the economy. The state is also involved since, for all the difficulties of public finance, the major institutions through which the savings of most people are channelled enjoy a privileged tax status.

PAY

7.19 The state has an interest in seeing a more moderate pay advance in the traded sectors of the economy, but this is not an easily secured, or sustained, objective. The state's interest in pay moderation comes both from a concern with international aspects of trade and currency management and from the labour-intensive nature of many of the public services. If pay advances disproportionately there is increased difficulty in financing the public services, but if the state tries to hold back public service pay relative to pay in other sectors, it faces 'winters of discontent'.

7.20 At the same time the state has been driven, repeatedly, to raise the levels of direct and indirect taxation falling on earned incomes and not least on low levels of earned income. This therefore becomes part of the cumulative pressure that stimulates more 'pay push', or more sense of felt injustice over pay. Nor can it escape from these pressures by a general contraction of public expenditure in real terms, for this may further contract employment, lower revenue and raise expenditure on those displaced, while worsening standards of public provision and increasing social inequality. Few European governments in recent years have been consistently successful in sustaining a constructive set of policies in this area. The need for a national dialogue on pay and economic priorities is all the greater if additional resources are to be directed to job creation and to the reduction of unemployment in both private and public sectors.

PUBLIC FINANCE AND BUSINESS

7.21 In its dealings with the rest of the economy, and the agencies and organisations through which economic activity and organisational power are influenced, the state is particularly affected by its public financial concerns. On occasion it wants to induce particular patterns of market behaviour (for example, to stimulate more industrial development and to moderate pay costs), or to reduce rates of price inflation. At the same time it wants to raise extensive tax revenues, which may directly or indirectly affect price levels and provoke compensatory responses from business or labour. It is also a large-scale borrower in the money markets, and therefore its activities affect more widely flows of investment funds, the availability of credit and the levels of interest rates. The problems of public finance would have been considerably more severe had it not been for the rapid rise in oil revenues to the state in the early 1980s. These revenues are now levelling out and are likely to fall in real terms later in the decade. Consequently, attempts at a constructive financial and economic dialogue with other participants in the market economy have to evolve against a background of constrained public finance. Attention has already been drawn to the adverse shift in the ratios of participation in the market economy compared with the (rising) proportion of the active population whose work, or unemployment, is financed by state directed transfers. These pressures will not disappear.

TRANSNATIONAL BUSINESS

7.22 The tension in relationships with business are particularly apparent in dealing with internationally mobile enterprises. The largest and most technically advanced firms play a major role in sustaining or developing the international competitiveness of UK-based industry and commerce. One hundred manufacturing firms generate over two-thirds of UK exports of manufactures and one hundred firms account for well over 90 per cent of industrial spending on research and development. But such firms operate increasingly as diversified and transnational enterprises. As world trade becomes more internationally inter-dependent the choices of development strategy open to such firms do not necessarily include development of the home economy. Instead, expectations of slow domestic growth, of an overvalued currency, or of other constraints on profitability may direct resources to other parts of the world.

7.23 As the crises of production and profitability developed in the 1970s, the state tried to shelter industrial firms from the storm by reducing tax liabilities and introducing new subsidies for industrial development. But that has further eroded the tax base which the state can draw on for all its activities. In recent years the state has become caught up in what is often explicit bargaining and lobbying over such development. A recent example has been the change in tax provisions as they affect North Sea oil. Such discussions have involved bargaining over the provision of selective aid and have proved relatively expensive for a weak economy anxiously seeking to capture more inward investment and to stimulate the growth of existing productive capacity. Wider questions of equity in the treatment of different firms competing in the same markets have also been raised. Such relationships have to take account of European Community rules and requirements designed to limit the extent to which member states can manipulate the conditions of competition. The European Community wll have to play a more important part in establishing the responsibilities of transnational companies across its member countries. But for some time to come the social urgency of encouraging more UK-based industrial development will ensure that the state will have to be involved in this development dialogue and in the trade-offs that become necessary.

PROTECTION

7.24 In face of all these constraints on the management of resources and finance, the state may seek to pull economic development forward at home at the expense of other countries and their workers. Earlier development of demand management by the state rested at least in part on the relatively closed and protectionist nature of national economies in the early post-war years. A stimulus to demand in the domestic economy did not 'leak' on such a large scale into higher imports or reduced exports, unless the economy was working at full capacity. The domestic stimulus could be combined with sufficient 'beggar my neighbour' policies (constraining imports and stimulating exports) to concentrate growth at home.

7.25 By contrast, a combination of an open and unprotected economy and areas of competitive weakness in domestic industry, would pose problems for any attempt to pursue growth through boosting domestic demand. Under these conditions, characteristic of the British economy in the 1970s and more recently, an increase in domestic spending power may well leak into disproportionate increases in imports (especially of manufactured goods). Thus in 1982 the first beginnings of a cyclical revival in consumer demand for durable and other consumer goods led to a disproportionate rise in manufactured imports and the share they took of the home market. The ratio of imports to home demand for manufactures rose from 24.3 per cent in 1981 to 28.5 per cent in 1982 (*British Business*, 21 January 1983). If imports had merely risen in line with home demand, UK manufacturing output would have risen three per cent. Instead, it fell by one per cent as imports increased their share of the home market.

7.26 Increasingly, international obligations have limited protection of the home economy (by limiting tariffs or restricting quota limitations on imports), especially for the UK in its trading relations with the other European Community members. In the Community as a whole most forms of protectionism between members have been eliminated. In important respects sovereignty over foreign trade relations is shared.

EXCHANGE RATES

7.27 The state may still, however, seek to secure a major shift in its competitiveness and its comparative costs by a substantial alteration in the exchange rate of its currency. Earlier international rules which sought to limit such changes to cases where it was generally agreed there was a fundamental imbalance in trade and underlying costs, have long since broken down. In consequence there is no guarantee that one country's devaluation will not be followed by those of other countries. Thus, in Europe in 1982 and 1983 there have been, in effect, major devaluations by France, Sweden, Spain, the UK and others.

7.28 Indeed, the UK has seen major devaluations of its currency timed to assist recovery from the depression phase of successive business cycles. This has been true of the last four such cycles (late 1967, 1972, 1976 and 1983–4). Such a stimulus can add opportunities of increased export volume as a spur to home industries at the same time as imports are checked by their increased costs in terms of the domestic currency. Although the benefits of such currency shifts come at the expense of other nations, they can be eroded by responses in the domestic economy, as well as by competitive devaluation elsewhere. Producers may prefer to raise prices to restore their profit margins, rather than pursue an aggressive policy of rebuilding market share. The British experience of devaluation has been that the cost advantages have not lasted for long and that subsequently trading weakness has returned.

7.29 More recent experience of operating the UK economy with a heavily overvalued exchange rate, as in the period from 1980 to mid 1981, has been even more depressing. Partly as a result in Britain's changed status as an oil producer in a period of oil crisis and partly through other measures such as comparatively high interest rates, the sterling exchange rate appreciated nearly 20 per cent against other currencies. At the same time the internal inflation rate was running around four per cent a year higher than that of other major trading economies. The consequence was manufacturing depression with a steep decline in output and a subsequent rapid deterioration in the trading balance in manufactures, as we have already indicated.

7.30 It may be that none of these responses to currency shifts was inevitable. But they have dominated the last fifteen years or so, and at the end of that period manufacturing output stands no higher than it did at the beginning.

A Shared Approach

7.31 The unilateral authority of the contemporary nation state is thus heavily constrained. The notion of effective 'sovereign' or command-giving powers in the international economy is a frustrating one in practice. A better strategy would be to pursue the opportunities of a shared and concerted approach to problems of employment and development, both internally and internationally. Institutions such as the European Community have a potential for the wider co-ordination of employment-creating policies which has not yet been fully tested. The Community's own agencies have, for example, been encouraging a co-ordinated approach to new patterns of work organisation and work-sharing. The dangers of trade imbalance as a barrier to national economic growth can be less acute if development is pursued in a more balanced and co-operative way by a larger group of trading nations. Since exchange rate policies are a matter of mutual concern it is better to seek to co-ordinate these and the associated internal policies of demand management, rather than to become trapped in competitive devaluations and other forms of trade retaliation.

LONGER TIME-SCALE

7.32 Too much state intervention has been taken up in an essentially short-run concern with the balancing of resources and demand. This is not to say that the state should not be concerned with the management of total levels of demand for resources. There is a need to be persistently concerned to reduce the under-employment of capital resources and the unemployment of people. But Britain now urgently needs a consistent and longer-term support for considered policies of development. The structural nature of many economic problems and the high risk and organisational upheaval involved in the painful task of adjustment to new circumstances need to be recognised. Such structural change does not flow readily from the signals of prices, costs, and profit expectations in the commercial world. It may also fail to be given due attention in a succession of state interventions concerned only with short-run elements of demand management.

LONGER-RUN POLICIES

7.33 Not only has policy direction been short-run. Lack of consensus has meant that it has been difficult to maintain any adequate continuity, even where this was attempted, in state aid to industrial re-organisation and development. The mechanisms of British political democracy have too often confined state action to short-run manipulation of the economy. This has been made more acute where other economic institutions have also worked with a very short time horizon in practice. Thus a good deal of 'City' investment in financial assets, including company equity shares, has hinged on short-run considerations of profit trends and short-run measures of the performance of invested funds. As to the important area of pay determination, in the same way the collective bargaining process has over many years been trapped inside agreements designed to last a mere twelve months. The energies of such institutions as these need to be directed towards a more constructive concern with the achievement of real long-term economic development in the UK. A conscious effort is needed to redirect many UK institutions towards this longer-run, forward-looking concern with the essential requirements of renewed economic development and a structural response to change. But it is not beyond the responsibility that can be asked both of the government and of the other institutions that command social influence and financial power.

7.34 To emphasise that there can be few costless solutions to economic problems calls for an exercise in responsibility rather than for despair. What it does mean is that it requires pain, effort and some sinking of vested interests to create the new opportunities, in the public and the private sector, for the constructive work and the wealth creation that Britain needs.

7.35 In the aftermath of many years of weak performance–particularly of manufacturing–and with the continuation of major structural changes in the economy, none of the organisations and institutions commanding economic resources, power and influence, should stand aside from an active and persistently supportive responsibility for renewed economic development. This would be reason enough for the emphasis in this chapter on shared responsibility, rather than unilateral assertion of power (whether coming from institutional hierarchies based on private property or on other hierarchies based on public property). But participation has to respect the needs of social justice too. It is not least the moral responsibility of the democratic state to make sure that what emerges is not participation in economic development by the 'haves' to the exclusion (from access to resources, and from influence over use of resources) of the 'have-nots'. Still less can the state clothe itself in moral authority if it presides over solutions in economic affairs on behalf of the 'haves' and at the expense of the 'have-nots'. Hence in moral terms the urgency or the centrality of the need to redesign not only economic development, but also working life and constructive social activity, so that all can contribute to, and share more fairly in, both wealth and welfare. With the lurch to massive long-term unemployment, there is a moral imperative on the democratic state, and that means on its citizens, not to 'pass by on the other side'.

Part Three

Reflections

Chapter Eight
A CHRISTIAN POINT OF VIEW

In the final chapter, which forms Part Three of the report, Peter Baelz comments on the arguments and themes of previous chapters and argues that the whole community shares a responsibility for meeting the basic needs of each of its members. He calls for long-term change in some basic attitudes.

Value Judgments

8.1 In the various chapters of this report a number of value judgments have been made or implied. Their authors have, for example, argued for more partnership, sharing, co-operation, responsibility and stewardship, all within the context of a changing world. The suggestion has been made that society be 'transformed' in accordance with such values, on the grounds that they are 'in keeping with', or 'pointing in the same direction as', the kingdom of God. It is the vision of the kingdom of God which gives the ultimate point of reference, but the implications of that vision have to be worked out afresh from within each new situation.

8.2 In the more immediate context of the British economy such 'transformation', it may be argued, does not call for a total and revolutionary change of existing structures. It is not unreasonable to hold that the changes which need to be made can and should be made on the basis of co-operation and consent. Such a view is not blind to the reality of powerful and conflicting interests, but it continues to believe and hope that in the existing situation they can still be made to serve a common good.

8.3 As a group we deliberately eschewed any attempt to arbitrate between the various economic schools of thought. We preferred to look more directly at the workings of three actual economic institutions without prior commitment to any particular theory or ideology. Nor was such commitment entailed by the theological model of 'transformation', since it does not rule out in advance either the necessity or the possibility of swift and radical change. Transformation, as such, may be swift or gradual–or, indeed, a combination of both. Nevertheless, in the present context, and for present purposes, the writer's own preference is to develop the model in terms of mediation and reconciliation rather than confrontation and revolution, paying greater regard to the biblical tradition of the 'Wisdom' literature than to that of Apocalyptic.

8.4 The structure of this report as a whole has been relatively simple. It began with a description of the work of the economist and the theologian. Next one of the members of our working group attempted an analysis of the major changes which have affected the economic scene since the end of the second world war. There then followed some account of the main schools of economic thought, their differing views of current economic difficulties and their divergent proposals for dealing with them. Behind these questions of economic policy deeper questions were indicated about the kind of society people wish to live in, and the need to set economic values within a wider context of fundamental social and human values.

8.5 From this base three central areas of economic life were selected for examination, the modern business enterprise, the community of work, and the state. Here description and evaluation began to emerge. We were concerned not only with understanding the situation in which Britain now finds itself, but also with suggesting the direction in which it ought to move forward.

THE INADEQUACY OF SHORT-TERM POLICIES

8.6 As a group, one of our basic contentions has been that *short-term and narrowly-conceived policies concerned only with immediate sectional interests are dangerously inadequate*. The temptation to invest time, energy and resources in programmes which promise a quick return and ignore both the wider community and the longer-term future is strong. It is, however, of vital importance that Britain should take up the challenge of developing new attitudes and accepting new responsibilities. Established institutions do not need to be destroyed, but they do need to be reshaped and re-directed, and this will be possible only if inherited, and now ill-adapted, categories of group interest and confrontation are transformed by a vision of a wider human community of co-operation and concern. Only such a vision, appealing to the combined sentiments of humanity and self-interest, can provide worthwhile longer-term goals, while at the same time sustaining people in the hardships which, at least in the shorter term, they will have to endure.

Christian Convictions

8.7 Let us turn now to say something more about the theological and ethical convictions that may help to shape a Christian approach. The question to be asked is: What specifically Christian contribution can there be to analysis and judgment in these matters?

8.8 Christians have their own way of perceiving and responding to the world in which they live. It is based on faith in God the Father of Jesus Christ and openness to his living Spirit. Although their value judgments will sometimes correspond with the judgments of others who do not profess the Christian faith, nevertheless their Christian commitment and their consequent beliefs about what makes for human wholeness and well-being give them a fundamental orientation and point of view from which to survey and interpret the economic scene.

8.9 Our remarks can be divided into three distinct, though overlapping, sections: first, the *context* in which Christians set economic life and activity; secondly, the *motivation* to which they make appeal; and thirdly, the *substance* of what they propose in the way of objectives and goals. In each of these sections it will be necessary to be selective.

THE CONTEXT OF ECONOMIC LIFE

8.10 The context in which Christians set economic life and activity is that of a world which is the sphere and object of God's continuing creative and redemptive love. Thus, the human economy is perceived as part and parcel of the divine economy. The material basis of human life is something God-given, and God is concerned with his human creatures' integral well-being, material and spiritual, individual and social. It is a mistake to draw a hard-and-fast line between the material and the spiritual, or between the individual and the social. The individual's natural concern for his or her own material needs may become disproportionate and selflsh, but concern for the material needs of others may be an act of spiritual service. To affirm, as Christians must, that spiritual values are more fundamental and enduring than material values is not to deny material values their rightful place in the hierarchy of human goods. It is, rather, to point out that they must not be given an importance beyond that which they can bear. 'What does a man gain by winning the whole world at the cost of his true self?' This said, however, Christians claim that economic activity and endeavour, the development and use of material resources for the common good of all, is a form of Christian obedience and service. Those involved in such activity are responsible to God for their part in the making, or marring, of the world.

8.11 Because the world is God's world, and man's life in the world is to be an expression of his response to God, Christian responsibility in economic affairs cannot be contained within nicely defined boundaries. Love of neighbour is, like God's love, inclusive rather than exclusive, reaching out to the poor and needy, whoever and wherever they may be, and so is incompatible with beggar-my-neighbour policies which seek success at the expense of others or mortgage the future to satisfy the excessive demands of the present. Nevertheless, there are limits, natural and human, to what human beings may hope to achieve. To say that choices are restricted because economic life is governed by impersonal economic forces is not to subscribe to a rigid determinism, but it is to recognise the complexity and, in part, the unpredictability of economic pressures. Even so, these forces are not totally opaque to human understanding, nor totally outside human control. Human beings are not their slaves. Faith in God, allied to prudence and foresight, calls for responsive and responsible action to meet basic human needs. Moreover, where resources are limited, and needs are many, efficiency becomes a moral economic virtue, a symbol of good stewardship.

8.12 Human nature itself gives rise to certain limits. Made in the image of God, but alienated from the life of God, human beings are both creative and destructive. On the one hand, they are what they are–that is, what nature and history, education and culture, have made them, the products of the past. On the other hand, they are also potentially what God calls them to become–his children and fellow-workers, inheritors of his kingdom, partakers of his holy Spirit. As sinners, they need to be constrained by law in order to protect and further the common good. Thus, they are subject to the power of the state. But this power is neither self-justifying nor ultimate. It too comes under the judgment of God, declared in the powerlessness of the Cross and the reality of the Resurrection.

8.13 The coming of God, foreshadowed and expressed in the person and teaching of Jesus, in his death and resurrection, destroys any illusion of a utopia guaranteed by human progress, the march of history or the triumph of the dialectic. At the same time, however, it gives shape and direction to human endeavour and is the source of a more than human hope. A Christian involvement in economic affairs should be both realistic and hopeful.

THE MOTIVATION FOR ECONOMIC ACTIVITY

8.14 When economic life is set within the wider context of the kingdom of God, the purpose of economic activity is transformed. It is now no longer solely an affair of the market, with individuals and groups seeking to satisfy as many of their own wants as they can. The emphasis shifts from wants to needs, and from the needs of the few to the needs of the many. Because men and women are now acknowledged to be members of a single human family, children of the one heavenly Father, they can begin to identify with each other and recognise the needs of others as their needs. Thus self-interest, which initially provides a check upon selfishness and a concern for the well-being of others on the insecure basis that 'if we do not hang together we shall all hang separately', now begins to draw on a deepening sense of a *common* destiny and a *common* good. The natural sentiment of humanity, fragile as it is, now finds deeper and stronger roots in God's care and concern for all mankind.

8.15 Self-interest may take people so far, but however 'enlightened', it is not enough, and Christian discipleship calls for a sacrificial love of neighbour and a willingness 'to go the extra mile'. Such self-forgetfulness is characteristic, not so much of a conscientious sense of duty as of an out-going care and concern. It is exemplified in the person of Jesus and grounded in the being of God.

8.16 Moral exhortation, addressed to the intellect and will, no doubt has a place in drawing human beings out of the narrow circle of their own selfish interests. Fortunately men and women have a capacity for co-operation on other than merely self-centred considerations. Nevertheless, *morality needs to be rooted in a vision of what truly is and what truly might be.* Thus the Christian vision of the kingdom of God gives another dimension and a profounder motivation to the search for prosperity along with justice and peace. Obedience to God, a sense of stewardship over his world and co-operation in his creative and redemptive work, all help to shape the basic attitude with which a Christian should engage in the economic life of the community. Competition between individuals and groups is not in itself incompatible with a Christian motivation. Indeed, it can be a form of co-operation and can harness human energy and resolve. But it needs to be contained within *a context of co-operation* in which there are agreed values and objectives. Otherwise, it degenerates into undisguised selfishness and unrestricted conflict.

DIFFERENCES OF ECONOMIC POLICY

8.17 When we turn from context and motivation to matters of substance, we enter a more problematic area. There is no simple or straightforward application of the Christian vision to a particular problem. A Christian judgment arises out of the interplay between the compelling vision and the immediate situation. There has to be a careful regard for the complexities of contingent circumstances. What is possible, however, is to be determined, not merely by the constraints of the past, but also by the potentialities of the future, a future which may be transformed by the power of the kingdom of

God. Even so, those who share the same vision of the kingdom can easily find themselves in disagreement when it comes to particular decisions. There may be a large measure of agreement about the direction in which to go, but judgments will differ about the immediate turning to take. Agreed objectives and goals do not necessarily imply agreed policies and proposals. The further people move from principles and objectives towards policies and particular courses of action, the more room there is for uncertainty and disagreement.

FUNDAMENTAL CRITERIA

8.18 The vision of the kingdom of God prescribes certain fundamental criteria for evaluating the goals and objectives of a fully human society. In God's kingdom there is a universal peace and harmony, combining justice and prosperity in a truly personal and fulfilling community. Its universality puts in question any social or economic system which allows the world to be divided into the powerful and the powerless, the rich and the poor, or allows one group of people, whether a class, a nation or a group of nations, to pursue its own welfare at the expense of the welfare of others. Its harmony and justice stem from the recognition that persons have a fundamental dignity of their own, independently of what they achieve or fail to achieve. *Thus the whole community shares a responsibility for meeting the basic needs of each of its members, while each of its members accepts his or her own responsibility for contributing to the common good of all.* Such a community is incompatible with an unbridled individualism, which in the name of freedom allows an inequitable access to material and human resources. It is also incompatible with an unchecked collectivism, which in the name of equality and the good of the majority exercises an ever more rigid control over the thoughts and actions of its members. Neither freedom nor equality represents an absolute value. Both need to be set within a context of fraternity, which stresses the givenness of a relationship of mutual belonging prior to any relationship based solely on shared interests.

8.19 The dynamic in the kingdom of God is shared care and concern, reflecting the indiscriminate love of God himself. This love is directed towards the meeting of human needs, both material needs, such as food and shelter, but also spiritual needs, such as freedom, responsibility and creativity.

A Just, Participatory and Sustainable Society

8.20 The values and dynamic of the kingdom of God cannot be translated directly into an economic programme and policy. As we have stressed earlier, not all men and women share these values, nor is the dynamic of love the only dynamic which motivates human action. Moreover, there are limits to human knowledge and ability as well as to natural resources. But they can suggest to us the kind of society which we must move towards if we wish to preserve and foster truly human values. It will be a society in which all its members count and have a place and identity of their own, because they are God's creatures and they all count in his sight. It will also be a society in which there is a fellowship of shared concern and responsibility, like that of the family of God. We might call such a society, in a phrase developed in the social thinking of the World Council of Churches, *a just, participatory and sustainable society*. If it is to be just, it must not allow inequalities, of whatever kind, to militate against that fundamental human dignity which belongs of right to all members, whatever their natural endowment and their individual attainment. If it is to be participatory, it must encourage its members freely to accept responsibility, not only for their own lives, but also for the ordering of the society and the institutions to which they belong. If it is to be sustainable, it must both create wealth for the present and preserve resources for the future.

8.21 If Christians agree that they must work for such a just, participatory and sustainable society, this agreement about goals and objectives still does not tell them how to solve the specific economic problems with which they are faced. To what extent, for example, is it right to appeal to individuals' and groups' self-interest rather than to their concern for the common good if, by so doing, significantly greater wealth can be created, some of which can then be used for social purposes? The 'profit motive' may provide the strongest incentive for creating wealth. It may, even, by satisfying widespread demands, contribute to the happiness of a large number of people. But it may also encourage a more general and sinister self-interest, if not selfishness, and this may loosen the cement of society, namely, its members' mutual trust and willingness to co-operate. It has been argued that there is a moral contradiction at the heart of 'free enterprise', in that it destroys the very virtues on which its success ultimately depends. On the other hand, if the power of the state is used to plan the allocation of natural resources and the direction of the economy in order to remove those inequalities which are socially divisive, a widespread spirit of passive dependence may be encouraged and the element of self-involvement, responsibility and participation which is also sought may be destroyed. There is no escape, within a given context, from making difficult judgments of priority and balance, nor is there any *a priori* rule for determining what these judgments should be.

CHANGES IN ATTITUDE

8.22 It seems that, if Britain is to rise to the challenges with which it is confronted by the present economic state of affairs, it must seek a long-term change in some basic attitudes. A deep sense of human dignity and worth which is not tied to economic achievement needs to be fostered. Undoubtedly, paid employment plays an important part in the lives of many people, in establishing their sense of worth. This is what makes involuntary unemployment so destructive and provides the motive for the demand for full employment. But living is more than working for a wage. Attention must be given to other aspects of human life, such as education, leisure, unpaid work and service, which, together with paid work, can contribute to the sense of human dignity. If, as seems likely, the dominant rhythms of paid work, as traditionally understood, are not going to be recovered, then it is all the more important that human *worth* should not be linked to what a person is paid. There are other forms of creativity which must be recognised as such. Furthermore, new patterns of community living need to be evolved which will give men and women a sense of individual worth and of importance to the community whether they are young or old, healthy or ill, in work or out of work. Hardships will continue to exist, and some will have more to cope with than others. But no-one should be allowed to reach the point where hardship, of whatever kind, threatens to become a diminution of his or her essential humanity.

8.23 In fostering such communities the state, alongside other institutions and groups, will have an important part to play. The question concerning the function of the state, whether it should be maximal or minimal, must be asked in different terms. The state is not the source or goal of human community, nor is it to be identified with the community. It is an instrument, indeed an essential instrument, for *developing* community. In order to carry out this function in the economic sphere it must play a positive but restricted role. It should neither monopolise nor abandon power. With careful regard to the changes which are happening it should take steps to ensure that there is a *creative long-term response* to these changes. It should seek to encourage and facilitate a growth of responsibility and a sense of trusteeship in the agencies of economic development. It should act against those inequalities which are destructive of community life and ensure that no section of society is debarred from fair access to resources. In the short-term it should protect the human dignity of all upon whom the processes of change and adjustment have brought suffering.

8.24 Britain needs to foster the sense that the efficient creation of material wealth can itself be a social service. At the same time it needs to learn that together with the creation of wealth must go the stewardship of wealth. In tomorrow's world co-operative skills will be as important as, if not more important than, competitive skills, and a greater emphasis must be placed on the need and the capacity to establish a co-operative commonwealth. *No amount of material wealth can justify a divided and unjust society, or a world divided into permanent haves and have-nots.*

8.25 Everyone must learn to look, not only to the wider world, but also to the future. There is a longer term as well as a shorter term responsibility, and the claims of the future must not be forgotten when the use of natural resources or areas of new investment are being considered. Thus a concern for the conservation as well as for the production and distribution of wealth needs to be developed.

8.26 Lastly, the distinction between human needs and human wants should be kept clear. Social institutions and a style of personal life should be encouraged which develop the wider range of human values and keep in check the impetus to go for ever higher levels of material production and consumption for some if this is at the expense of others.

8.27 If these are some of the attitudes and objectives which need to be developed for there to be a creative response to the demands of the present economic state of affairs, what courses of action are most likely to further these attitudes and attain these objectives? In earlier chapters members of our group have made a number of suggestions, which arise out of an interplay between the convictions summarised in this chapter and an understanding of the present situation. These suggestions are, however, only a beginning. There remains a gap between theological reflection and economic prescription, a gap of which we in our working group were acutely aware but which admittedly we have not bridged. Had we more time and patience, it is possible that we could have agreed on some more specific economic recommendations. On the other hand, as has been suggested more than once, the nature of this gap may be such that it cannot logically be 'bridged'. Economic recommendations are as much about means as they are about ends, and it is the situation rather than the theology which largely determines the appropriateness of means. Even where the question is one about objectives and ends, Christians may not, in a world in which values are not all immediately compatible, come to a common mind. In responding to a particular situation there is room for the immediate insight of the prophet as well as the continuing tradition of the professor, and there is room for the common sense of the ordinary Christian disciple as well as the more special gifts of both professor and prophet. If as a working group we have achieved anything, it has been to draw a kind of map and point a number of directions. It still remains for the route to be planned. In this planning those with practical experience as well as those with professional expertise, Christians together with men and women of good will, have a work to accomplish and a service to render.

FOR FURTHER READING

Other reports and papers from the Industrial and Economic Affairs Committee offer additional discussion of some of the matters raised in *Perspectives on Economics* and may be of interest:

Reports

Transnational Corporations: Confronting the Issues. April 1983. 80 pages. CIO Publishing. £2.20.

Seven essays concentrating on the nature of the impact of TNCs in the third world and the problems caused for organised labour in the developed countries.

Winters of Discontent: Industrial Conflict—A Christian Perspective. May 1981. 60 pages. CIO Publishing. £1.75.

A study of industrial conflict examining the characteristics of industrial society and industry's main groupings.

Work and the Future: Technology, World Development and Jobs in the Eighties. November 1979. 44 pages. CIO Publishing. £1.

An analysis of the experience of work and the impact of new technology, together with a moral perspective and the need for experiment with new forms of organisation.

Working Papers

Christian Ethics and Christian Social and Political Action: Some American Themes. March 1984. 37 pages. 50 pence.

Democracy in Trade Unions: A Submission to Government. June 1983. 5 pages. 35 pence.

Unemployment and the Future of Work: Study Pack. December 1982. 45 pages. 70 pence.

Industrial Relations Legislation: Comments from the Industrial Committee. February 1982. 15 pages. 30 pence.

Energy Questions. November 1980. 33 pages. 25 pence.

The Ethical Use of Investment Funds. July 1980. 14 pages. 20 pence.

Reports are available through any bookshop (or from the Church House Bookshop, Great Smith Street, London SW1). Working Papers are available from the Industrial Committee, Room 463, Church House, Dean's Yard, London SW1. A full list of current Industrial Committee publications is available on request.

MEMBERS OF THE WORKING GROUP

The Very Revd Peter Baelz*

Dean of Durham, formerly Regius Professor of Moral and Pastoral Theology, the University of Oxford (Chairman)

Mr Donald Hay

Fellow and Tutor in Economics, Jesus College, Oxford

Mr John Hughes

Principal, Ruskin College, Oxford

Professor John Pickering*†§

Professor of Industrial Economics, the University of Manchester Institute of Science and Technology

Mr Douglas Todd§

Economic Adviser, Directorate-General for Economic and Financial Affairs, Commission of the European Communities, formerly Senior Economic Adviser, HM Treasury

The Revd Paul Brett

Secretary, Industrial and Economic Affairs Committee of the Board for Social Responsibility (Secretary)

(The symbol * indicates a member of the General Synod, † a member of the Board for Social Responsibility, and § a member of the Board's Industrial and Economic Affairs Committee.)

All the above have acted in a private capacity and not as representatives of the organisations mentioned. The views expressed are those of the Working Group, or of the authors named, as applicable. They should not necessarily be thought to represent the opinions of anyone else.